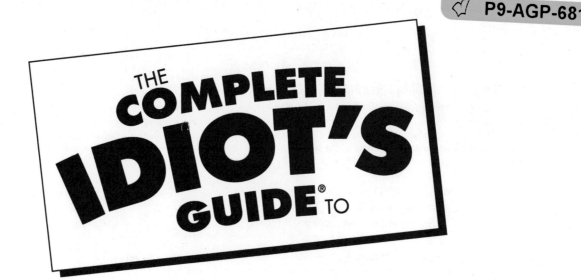

THE COMPLETE IDIOT'S GUIDE® TO

Acoustic Guitar Songs

A copublication of Alfred Publishing Co., Inc. and Penguin Group (USA) Inc.

Alfred Publishing Co., Inc.

International Standard Book Number: 978-0-7390-4627-2
Library of Congress Catalog Card Number: 2007924613

09 08   8 7 6 5 4 3

Interpretation of the printing code: The rightmost number of the first series of numbers is the year of the book's printing; the rightmost number of the second series of numbers is the number of the book's printing. For example, a printing code of 07-1 shows that the first printing occurred in 2007.

Printed in the United States of America

Published under agreement by Alfred Publishing Co., Inc.

Distributed by Alfred Publishing Co., Inc. and Penguin Group (USA) Inc. All rights reserved.

Alpha Books
Publisher: *Marie Butler-Knight*
Editorial Director/Acquiring Editor: *Mike Sanders*
Managing Editor: *Billy Fields*
Senior Development Editor: *Phil Kitchel*
Senior Production Editor: *Janette Lynn*
Design and Layout: *Becky Harmon, Brian Massey*
Proofreader: *Aaron Black*

Alfred Publishing
Publishers: *Steven Manus and Ron Manus*
Editor-in-Chief: *L. C. Harnsberger*
Project Managers: *Aaron Stang and Kate Westin*
Senior Editor: *Kate Westin*
Instructional Text: *Jack Allen and Aaron Stang*
Biographical Text: *Jon Senge and Donny Trieu*
Engraving Manager: *Al Nigro*

Contents

Artist Index

Introduction

We all play guitar for pretty much the same reason—to play our favorite songs. It's so easy to get caught up in mastering technique, learning to read music, or understanding music theory that we can spend hours at the instrument and still not have a good song to play. Note reading, technique, and theory are all great tools—but that's all they are. This is your chance to put all those tools together to play songs!

Learning all your favorite songs is the single most important musical learning experience you can have. All the songs in this book use related chords, scales, techniques, and other elements, so as you learn your favorite songs, you are actually learning the skills you need to play other favorites as well.

Everything is included to help you play every song. First, there is a review of the basics, like holding the guitar and reading music and TAB. Every song is then presented with a short introduction that explores the tricks to making it easy to play. All the music is shown in standard music notation, TAB, and guitar chords so you can choose which is best for you.

We suggest getting the recordings to all the songs in this book that you plan to learn. Listen to them often, and keep them handy as you learn each song. It's not important that you master every aspect of every song. You can focus on the parts that grab your attention the most—a lick you like, the melody, the chords, or just anything you *want* to play. As you gain experience, technique, and knowledge, putting the pieces together and learning the complete songs will get easier and easier.

Be sure to check out the other books in this series to see if there are other favorites you'd like to learn. If you want more information on playing the guitar, reading music, or even writing your own music, there are lots of other *Complete Idiot's Guides* to help you along.

Now tune your guitar, crank up the music, and dig in.

How to Use This Book

Some people approach learning an instrument by isolating all the technical skills, and through years of study and practice, develop a command of those skills and tools. Others learn simply by having a friend show them a simple song, and then proceed to learn on a song-by-song basis. Some combination of the two methods is probably the best, but you should always spend a good portion of your music time learning songs that you would really love to perform for your friends and family—or for yourself.

In this book, each song is written in full music notation and TAB (tablature). Reading music is a skill acquired through diligent practice, and it has many benefits. TAB offers a quick way of knowing what to play without having to be an accomplished music reader. We believe that providing TAB in conjunction with standard music notation is the ideal way to get you up and playing right away. All the guitar parts include TAB to show exactly where to fret each note. Guitar chord grids indicate chord fingerings for strumming and fingerpicking accompaniment parts.

Start by picking a song you really want to play. If you don't already have one, get a copy of the recording and listen to it carefully as you learn the song. Music is an aural art, so always have the sound of the song clearly in your head before you attempt to learn to play it on the guitar.

Read through the lesson that precedes each song and practice the example music before attempting to play the whole song. Each lesson is broken into various sections. We've also included some sidebars along the way to point out things that are particularly important, interesting, or helpful.

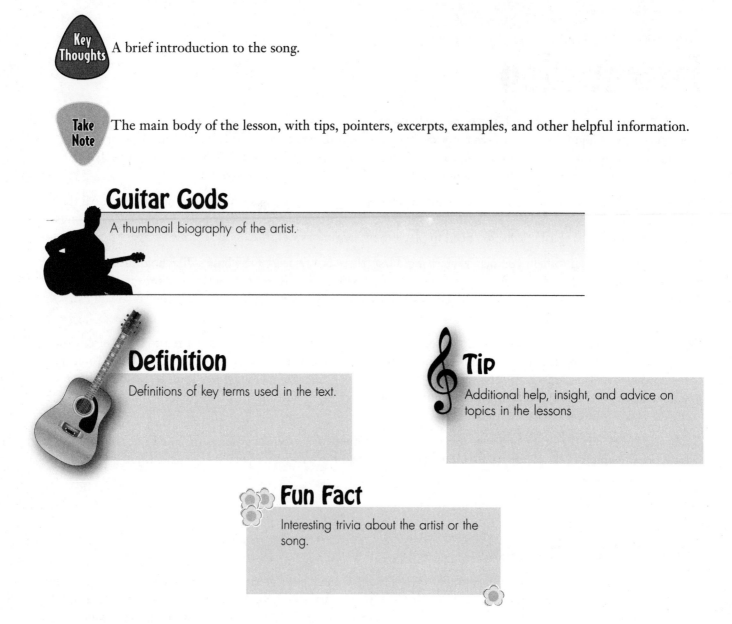

Key Thoughts A brief introduction to the song.

Take Note The main body of the lesson, with tips, pointers, excerpts, examples, and other helpful information.

Guitar Gods

A thumbnail biography of the artist.

Definition

Definitions of key terms used in the text.

Tip

Additional help, insight, and advice on topics in the lessons

Fun Fact

Interesting trivia about the artist or the song.

If you want to know more about chords, be sure to read Appendix A. It will teach you about the different kinds of chords, how they are constructed, and what the symbols mean.

Appendix B is a diagram of the guitar fretboard, showing every note on every string up to the twelfth fret.

Finally, we've provided a glossary in Appendix C that covers all the music terms used throughout this book.

Acknowledgments

Special thanks to the Alfred Publishing writing, editing, and arranging team of Jack Allen, Danny Begelman, Al Nigro, Jon Senge, Aaron Stang, Donny Trieu, and Kate Westin. Thanks also to James Grupenhoff and Marcus Thomas for licensing, and to Steve Manus, Ron Manus, and Link Harnsberger for initiating and supporting this project.

Trademarks

All terms mentioned in this book that are known to be or are suspected of being trademarks or service marks have been appropriately capitalized. Alpha Books/Penguin Group (USA) Inc. and Alfred Publishing Co., Inc. cannot attest to the accuracy of this information. Use of a term in this book should not be regarded as affecting the validity of any trademark or service mark.

Reviewing the Basics

Getting to Know Your Guitar

You may or may not be able to name all the parts of your guitar, and you may or may not need to. If you ever get into a conversation with another guitarist, however, it will probably go better if you know what is being referred to as "the nut" or "the bridge."

The Parts of the Guitar

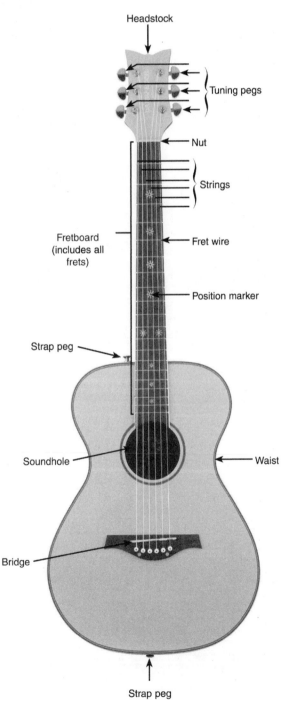

Headstock

Tuning pegs

Nut

Strings

Fretboard
(includes all
frets)

Fret wire

Position marker

Strap peg

Soundhole

Waist

Bridge

Strap peg

Steel Strings and Nylon Strings

Steel strings are found on both acoustic and electric guitars. They have a bright and brassy sound.

Nylon strings are usually found on classical and flamenco guitars. They have a mellow, delicate sound. Nylon strings tend to be easier on the fingers than steel strings.

How to Hold Your Guitar

Below are three typical ways of holding your guitar. Pick the one that is most comfortable for you.

Sitting.

Sitting with legs crossed.

Standing with a strap.

Using Your Right Hand

Sometimes your right hand will play individual notes on a single string, and sometimes it will play chords using many strings. To *strum* means to play several strings by brushing quickly across them, either with a pick or with your fingers. This is the most common way of playing a chord.

Strumming with a Pick

Hold the pick between your thumb and index finger. Hold it firmly, but don't squeeze too hard.

On a *down-stroke*, strum from the lowest note of the chord to the highest note of the chord. Move mostly your wrist, not just your arm. For an *up-stroke*, strike the strings from highest to lowest.

Tip

Strumming is done mostly from the wrist, not the arm. Use as little motion as possible. Start as close to the string as you can, and never let your hand move past the edge of the guitar.

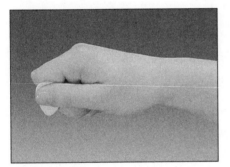

Holding the pick.

Starting near the lowest string.

Finishing near the highest string.

Strumming with Your Fingers

First, decide if you feel more comfortable strumming with the side of your thumb or with the nail of your fingers. The strumming motion is the same with the thumb or fingers as it is when using the pick.

Strumming with the thumb.

Strumming with the fingers.

Using Your Left Hand

Your left hand needs to be relaxed when you play. It's also important to keep your fingernails neat and trim so that your fingers will curve in just the right way, otherwise you'll hear lots of buzzing and muffling.

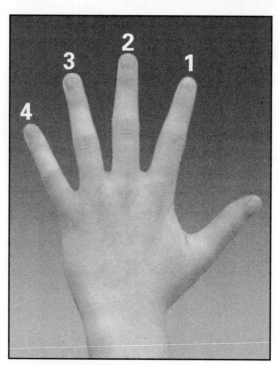

The left hand finger numbers.

Proper Left Hand Position

Your left hand fingers will work best when your hand is correctly shaped and positioned. Place your hand so your thumb rests comfortably in the middle of the back of the neck and your wrist is away from the fingerboard. Position your fingers on the front of the neck as if you are gently squeezing a ball between them and your thumb. Keep your elbow in and your fingers curved.

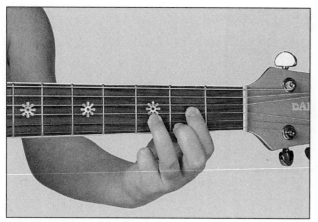

Front view.

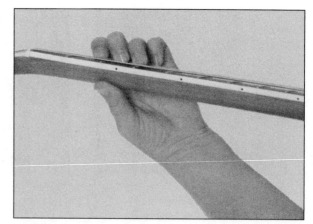

Top view.

Placing a Finger on a String

When you press a string with a left hand finger, make sure you press firmly with the tip of your finger and as close to the fret wire as you can without actually being right on it. This will create a clean, bright tone. If your finger is too far from the fret wire, the note will buzz. If it is on top of the fret wire, you'll get a muffled, unclear sound. Also, make sure your finger stays clear of neighboring strings.

Right! The finger is close to the fret wire.

Wrong! The finger is too far from the fret wire.

Wrong! The finger is on top of the fret wire.

Tuning Your Guitar

Every musician knows the agony of hearing an instrument that is not in tune. Always be sure to tune your guitar every time you play, and check the tuning every now and then between songs.

About the Tuning Pegs

First, make sure your strings are wound properly around the tuning pegs. They should go from the inside to the outside as shown in the illustration. Turning a tuning peg clockwise makes the pitch lower. Turning a tuning peg counter-clockwise makes the pitch higher. Be sure not to tune the strings too high, or you run the risk of breaking them.

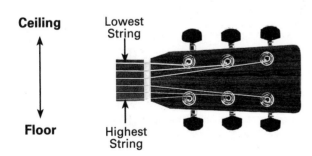

Ceiling

Floor

Lowest String

Highest String

 Tip

Always remember that the thinnest, highest-sounding string, the one closest to the floor, is the *1st* string. The thickest, lowest-sounding string, the one closest to the ceiling, is the *6th* string. When guitarists say "the top string," they are referring to the highest-sounding string, and "the bottom string" is the lowest-sounding string.

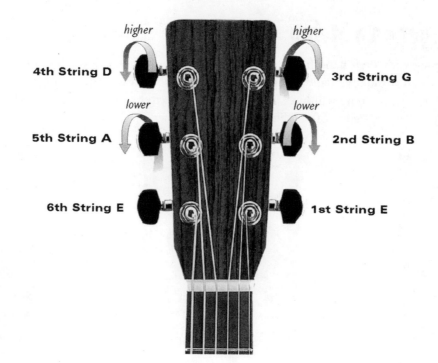

Tuning the Guitar to Itself

When your 6th string is in tune, you can tune the rest of the strings using the guitar by itself. The easiest way to tune the 6th string is with a piano. If you don't have a piano available, consider buying an electronic tuner or pitch pipe. There are many types available, and a salesperson at your local music store can help you decide which is best for you.

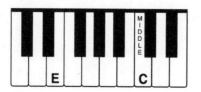

If you have access to a piano, tune the 6th string to the note E below middle C.

The 6th string is tuned to E below middle C.

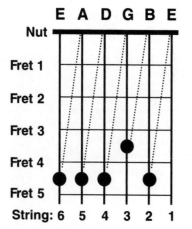

To tune the rest of the strings, follow this sequence:

- ◆ Press 5th fret of 6th string to get pitch of 5th string (A).
- ◆ Press 5th fret of 5th string to get pitch of 4th string (D).
- ◆ Press 5th fret of 4th string to get pitch of 3rd string (G).
- ◆ Press 4th fret of 3rd string to get pitch of 2nd string (B).
- ◆ Press 5th fret of 2nd string to get pitch of 1st string (E).

The Basics of Music Notation

Standard music notation contains a plethora of musical information. If you don't already read notation, you will probably benefit from studying the following fundamental concepts. Understanding even a little about reading notation can help you create a performance that is true to the original.

Notes

Notes are used to indicate musical sounds. Some notes are held long and others are short.

Note Values

whole note	𝅝	4 beats
half note	𝅗𝅥	2 beats
quarter note	𝅘𝅥	1 beat
eighth note	𝅘𝅥𝅮	½ beat
sixteenth note	𝅘𝅥𝅯	¼ beat

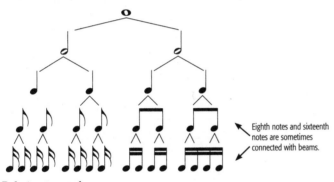

Eighth notes and sixteenth notes are sometimes connected with beams.

Relative note values.

When a *dot* follows a note, the length of the note is longer by one half of the note's original length.

Dotted Note Values

dotted half note	𝅗𝅥.	3 beats
dotted quarter note	𝅘𝅥.	1½ beats
dotted eighth note	𝅘𝅥𝅮.	¾ beat

A *triplet* is a group of three notes played in the time of two. Triplets are identified by a small numeral "3" over the note group.

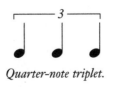

Quarter-note triplet.

Rests

Rests are used to indicate musical silence.

Rest Values

whole rest	▬	4 beats
half rest	▬	2 beats
quarter rest	𝄽	1 beat
eighth rest	𝄾	½ beat
sixteenth rest	𝄿	¼ beat

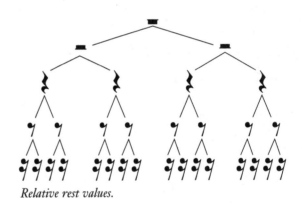

Relative rest values.

The Staff

Music is written on a *staff* made up of five lines and four spaces, numbered from the bottom up. Each line and space is designated as a different pitch.

line 5 → _____ ← space 4
line 4 → _____ ← space 3
line 3 → _____ ← space 2
line 2 → _____ ← space 1
line 1 →

7

The staff is divided into equal units of time called *measures* or *bars*.

Measure.

A *bar line* indicates where one measure ends and another begins.

Bar line.

A *double bar line*, made of one thin line and one thick line, shows the end of a piece of music.

Double bar line.

Notes on the Staff

Notes are named using the first seven letters of the alphabet (A B C D E F G). The higher a note is on the staff, the higher its pitch.

E F G A B C D E F

The *treble clef*, also called the *G clef*, is the curly symbol you see at the beginning of each staff. The treble clef designates the second line of the staff as the note G.

Here are the notes on the lines of the treble staff. An easy way to remember them is with the phrase "Every Good Boy Does Fine."

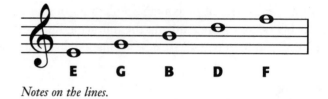

E G B D F

Notes on the lines.

Here are the notes on the spaces. They are easy to remember because they spell the word FACE.

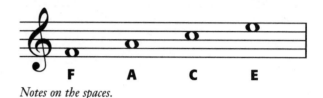

F A C E

Notes on the spaces.

The staff can be extended to include even higher or lower notes by using *ledger lines*. You can think of ledger lines as small pieces of additional staff lines and spaces. The lowest note in the following figure is the open low E string of the guitar.

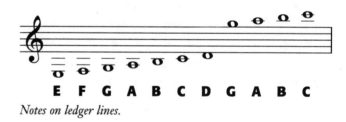

E F G A B C D G A B C

Notes on ledger lines.

Accidentals

An *accidental* raises or lowers the sound of a note. A *sharp* ♯ raises a note one *half step*, which is the distance from one fret to another. A *flat* ♭ lowers a note one half step. A *natural* ♮ cancels a sharp or a flat. An accidental remains in effect until the end of the measure, so if the same note has to be played flat or sharp again, only the first one will have the accidental. See the Guitar Fingerboard Chart on page 170 for all the flat and sharp notes on the guitar up to the 12th fret.

HALF STEPS • NO FRET BETWEEN

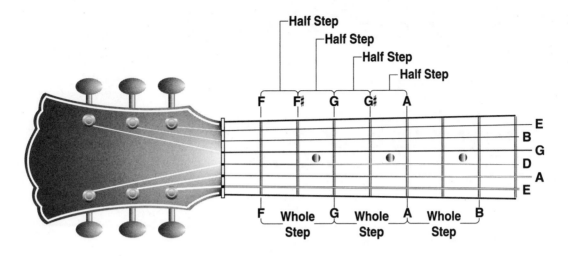

WHOLE STEPS • ONE FRET BETWEEN

Key Signatures

Sometimes certain notes need to be played sharp or flat throughout an entire song. In this case, it's easier to put the sharps or flats in the *key signature* instead of putting an accidental on each individual note. If you see sharps or flats at the beginning of a staff just after the treble clef, that means to play those notes sharp or flat throughout the music. The key signature can change within a song as well, so be sure to keep an eye out. Below are two examples of key signatures.

Play each F, C, and G as F♯, C♯, and G♯.

Play each B and E as B♭ and E♭.

Time Signatures

The *time signature* is a symbol resembling a fraction that appears at the beginning of the music. The top number tells you how many beats are in each measure, and the bottom number tells you what kind of note gets one beat. Most songs have the same number of beats in every measure, but the time signature can also change within a song. It's important to notice each time signature and count correctly, otherwise you could end up getting ahead in the song or falling behind.

4 (top) = 4 beats to a measure

4 (bottom) = quarter note ♩ gets 1 beat

C is a time signature that means the same as $\frac{4}{4}$.

9

3 = 3 beats to a measure
4 = quarter note ♩ gets 1 beat

6 = 6 beats to a measure
8 = eighth note ♪ gets 1 beat

9 = 9 beats to a measure
8 = eighth note ♪ gets 1 beat

12 = 12 beats to a measure
8 = eighth note ♪ gets 1 beat

Ties

A *tie* is a curved line that joins two or more notes of the same pitch, which tells you to play them as one continuous note. Instead of playing the second note, continue to hold for the combined note value. Ties make it possible to write notes that last longer than one measure, or notes with unusual values.

Hold B for five beats.

The Fermata

A *fermata* ⌒ over a note means to pause, holding for about twice as long as usual.

Pause on notes with a fermata.

Repeat Signs

Most songs don't start and then ramble on in one continuous stream of thought to the end. They are constructed with sections, such as verses and choruses, that are repeated in some organized pattern. To avoid having to go through pages and pages of duplicate music, several different types of *repeat signs* are used to show what to play again. Repeat signs act as a kind of roadmap, telling you when to go back and where to go next, navigating you through the song.

Repeat Dots

The simplest repeat sign is two dots on the inside of a double bar. It means to go back to the beginning and play the music over again.

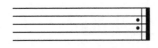

Go back and play again.

When just a section of music is to be repeated, an opposite repeat sign at the beginning of the section tells you to repeat everything in between.

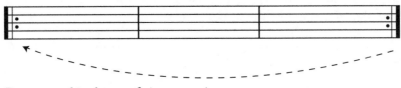

Repeat everything between facing repeat signs.

1st and 2nd Endings

When a section is repeated but the ending needs to be different, the *1st ending* shows what to play the first time, and the *2nd ending* shows what to play the second time. Play the 1st ending, repeat, then skip the 1st ending and play the 2nd ending.

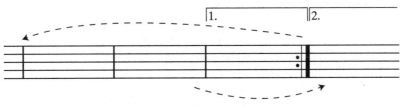

Play the 1st ending, repeat, then skip to the 2nd ending.

Other Repeat Signs

D.C. al Fine	Repeat from the beginning and end at ***Fine***.
D.C. al Coda	Repeat from the beginning and play to the coda sign ⊕, then skip to the ***Coda*** and play to the end.
D.S. al Fine	Repeat from the sign 𝄋 and end at ***Fine***.
D.S. al Coda	Repeat from the sign 𝄋 and play to the coda sign ⊕, then skip to the ***Coda*** and play to the end.

Reading Guitar Tablature (TAB)

Tablature, or *TAB* for short, is a graphic representation of the six strings of the guitar. Although standard notation gives you all the information you need to play a song, the TAB staff tells you quickly where to finger each note on the guitar. The bottom line of the TAB staff represents the 6th string, and the top line is the 1st string. Notes and chords are indicated by the placement of fret numbers on each string.

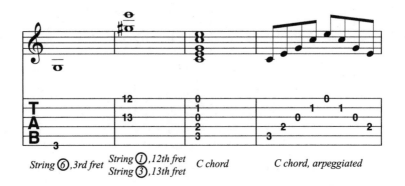

String ⑥, 3rd fret *String ①, 12th fret* *C chord* *C chord, arpeggiated*
String ③, 13th fret

The following are examples of various guitar techniques you might come across in the notation of the songs. Unless otherwise indicated, the left hand does the work for these.

Bending Notes

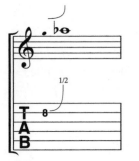

Half step: Play the note and bend the string one half step (the sound of one fret).

Slight bend/quarter-tone bend: Play the note and bend the string slightly sharp.

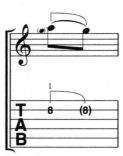

Prebend and release: Play the already-bent string, then immediately drop it down to the fretted note.

Whole step: Play the note and bend the string one whole step (the sound of two frets).

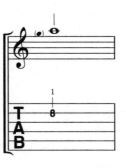

Prebend (ghost bend): Bend to the specified note before the string is plucked.

Unison bends: Play both notes and immediately bend the lower note to the same pitch as the higher note.

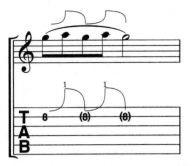

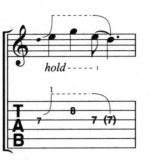

Bend and release: Play the note and bend to the next pitch, then release to the original note. Only the first note is attacked.

Bends involving more than one string: Play the note and bend the string while playing an additional note on another string. Upon release, relieve the pressure from the additional note, allowing the original note to sound alone.

Bends involving stationary notes: Play both notes and immediately bend the lower note up to pitch. Return as indicated.

Articulations

Hammer-on: Play the lower note, then "hammer" your left hand finger onto the string to sound the higher note. Only the first note is plucked.

Muted strings: A percussive sound is produced by striking the strings with the right hand while laying the fret hand across them.

Pull-off: Play the higher note with your first finger already in position on the lower note. Pull your finger off the first note with a strong downward motion that plucks the string, sounding the lower note.

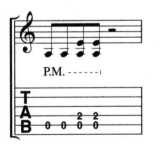

Palm mute: The notes are muted (muffled) by placing the palm of the right hand lightly on the strings, just in front of the bridge.

Legato slide: Play the first note, and with continued pressure applied to the string, slide up to the second note. The diagonal line shows that it is a slide and not a hammer-on or a pull-off.

Harmonics

Natural harmonic: Lightly touch the string with the fret hand at the note indicated in the TAB and pluck the string, producing a bell-like sound called a harmonic.

Artificial harmonic: Fret the note at the first TAB number, then use a right hand finger to lightly touch the string at the fret indicated in parentheses (usually 12 frets higher than the fretted note), and pluck the string with an available right hand finger or your pick.

Pick Direction

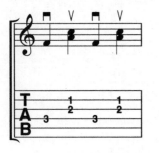

Down-strokes and up-strokes: The down-stroke is indicated with this symbol ⊓, and the up-stroke is indicated with this one ∨.

Rhythm Slashes

Strum marks with rhythm slashes: Strum with the indicated rhythm pattern. Strum marks can be located above the staff or within the staff.

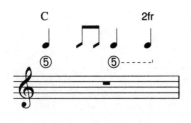

Single notes with rhythm slashes: Sometimes single notes are incorporated into a strum pattern. The note name is given, with the string number in a circle and the fret number indicated.

Big Yellow Taxi

Key Thoughts

Joni Mitchell has become one of the world's foremost proponents of *altered tunings*. An altered tuning is simply a different way of tuning one or more strings. Although playing in an altered tuning can be disorienting at first, it can also open the door to easy creative explorations and lead the way to new sonic possibilities on the guitar.

Take Note

"Big Yellow Taxi," from relatively early in Joni's career, is in *Open E tuning*. In Open E, each string on the guitar is tuned to one of the notes of an E major chord. Joni represents this tuning as E–7–5–4–3–5. This system tells you that the low 6th string is tuned to E, the open 5th string is tuned to the seventh fret of the 6th string, the open 4th string is tuned to the fifth fret of the 5th string, and so on.

Using open tunings on the guitar can present challenges, but it also creates opportunities. One major plus is that you can produce a chord simply by barring your finger across the fretboard in any position. Another advantage is that you can take the "conventional" chord fingerings from standard tuning and use them in an altered tuning to reveal delightful combinations of notes that would have been inconceivable in standard tuning.

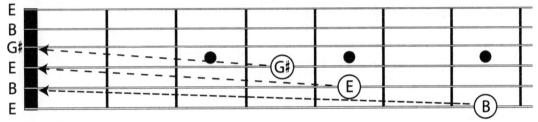

Open E tuning.

"Big Yellow Taxi" has three basic chords: E, A, and B, played in the open, fifth-fret, and seventh-fret positions, respectively, with an occasional embellishment on the open E chord. Happy strummin'!

Fun Fact

The first "Earth Day" was in 1970, the same year this song was published. At the dawn of the environmental movement, Joni Mitchell came up with this simple, light-hearted tune with a whimsical warning: "They paved paradise and put up a parking lot."

Acous. Gtr. in Open E tuning:
⑥ = E ③ = G♯
⑤ = B ② = B
④ = E ① = E

BIG YELLOW TAXI

Words and Music by
JONI MITCHELL

Moderately ♩ = 104

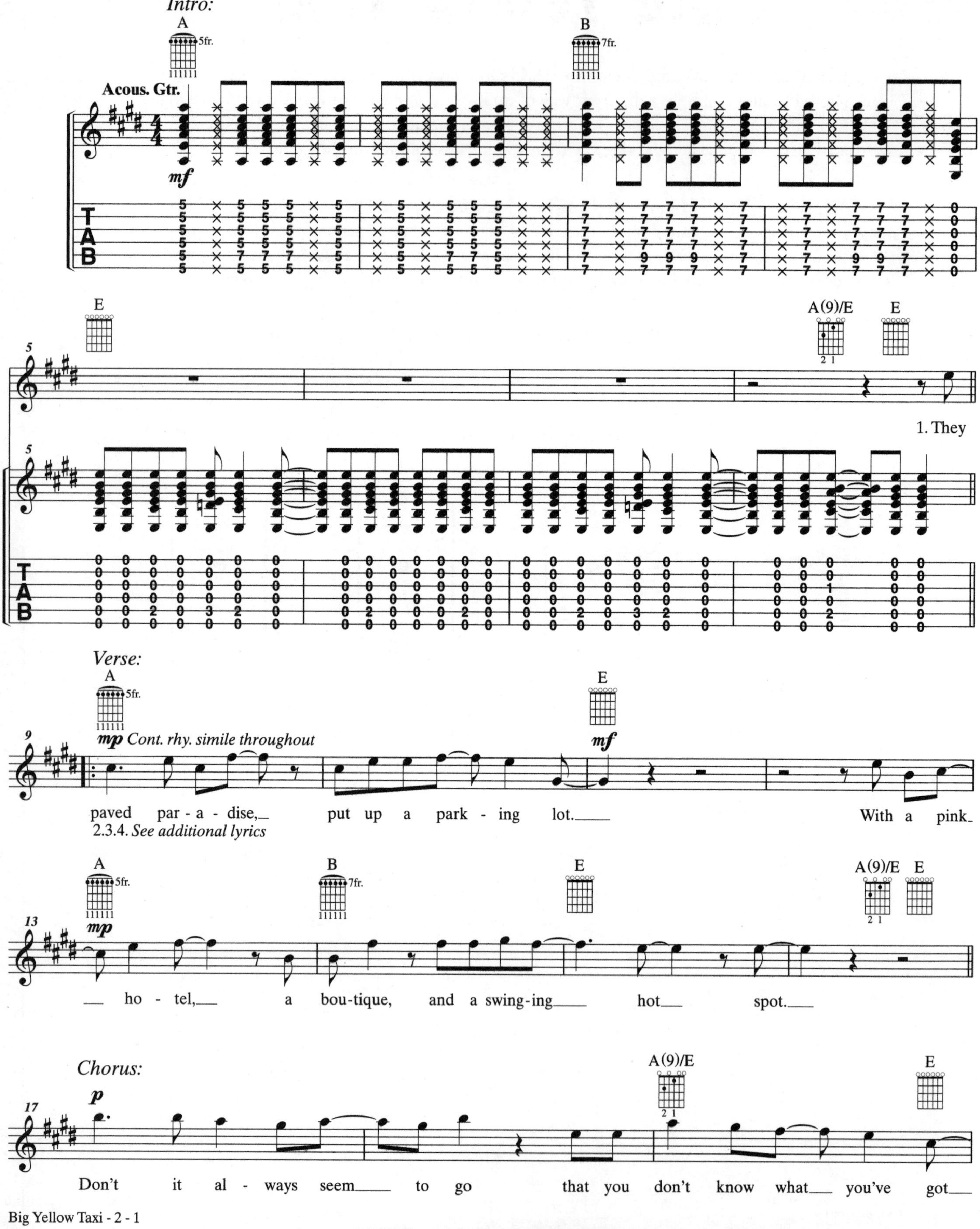

Intro:
A
5fr.
111111
B
7fr.
111111
Acous. Gtr.
mf
TAB
E
A(9)/E
21
E
1. They
Verse:
A
mp Cont. rhy. simile throughout
E
mf
paved par - a - dise,_ put up a park - ing lot.___ With a pink_
2.3.4. See additional lyrics
A
B
E
A(9)/E E
mp
___ ho - tel,___ a bou-tique, and a swing-ing___ hot___ spot.___
Chorus:
p
A(9)/E
E
Don't it al - ways seem___ to go that you don't know what___ you've got___

Big Yellow Taxi - 2 - 1

Verse 2:
They took all the trees,
Put 'em in a tree museum.
And they charged the people
A dollar and a half just to see 'em.
(To Chorus:)

Verse 3:
Hey farmer, farmer,
Put away that DDT now.
Give me spots on my apples,
But leave me the birds and the bees,
Please!
(To Chorus:)

Verse 4:
Late last night
I heard the screen door slam.
And a big yellow taxi
Took away my old man.
(To Chorus:)

Both Sides, Now

Key Thoughts Joni Mitchell plays "Both Sides, Now" with her guitar tuned in the same Open E altered tuning as "Big Yellow Taxi" (E B E G♯ B E). Although our version of the song is arranged in standard guitar tuning, we've used chords that emulate the fascinating sound of Joni's open tuning.

Take Note This song contains some very interesting chords such as the B/E chord, which combines notes of a B chord and an E chord together. The trick when playing both the B/E and the A/E is to *mute* the open 4th string, meaning to stop it from sounding. To do this, simply allow your 3rd finger, which is on the 5th string, to lean back and gently touch the 4th string to keep it from making a sound. The muted note is indicated with an "x" on the 4th string in the chord diagrams shown below.

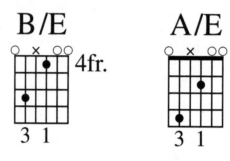

Guitar Gods

JONI MITCHELL is arguably the most influential female pop musician of all time. Everyone from Chrissie Hynde to Madonna to Courtney Love has been affected by Mitchell's insightful, groundbreaking music. Her career encompasses folk, pop, jazz, avant-garde, and even world music, but her creativity, more than anything else, is what sets her apart. She is a phenomenal songwriter and a trailblazer who chooses not to confine herself to any single musical style. Mitchell has changed her music in unprecedented ways and speeds. As a guitarist, she is wildly inventive, most notably in her innovative use of multiple tunings. Her work with musicians of various genres encompasses an extraordinary list of collaborators that reads like a virtual "who's who" in music, including Jaco Pastorius, Larry Carlton, Wayne Shorter, Chaka Khan, Charles Mingus, Peter Gabriel, Willie Nelson, Tom Petty, Billy Idol, David Crosby, Stephen Stills, and James Taylor.

Mitchell moved to the United States from Canada after signing with Reprise Records in 1967. Her debut was a self-titled acoustic effort that appeared the following year. From then on, she released a string of albums. Her song "Woodstock," which would later become a major hit for Crosby, Stills, Nash & Young, is featured on the 1970 album *Ladies of the Canyon*, along with "Big Yellow Taxi." Mitchell's landmark release was *Blue* in 1971, a brilliant, confessional album that firmly established her as one of music's most remarkable talents.

To get a good rhythmic flow that supports the melody, try to parallel the rhythm of the melody with your strum pattern. Also, try to alternate playing full-chord strums, bass notes, and occasional up-strums with just the top two strings on the "&" of beat 4 before changing to a new chord. The example below is written out in full notation and TAB to give you an idea of how this should all come together.

 Tip

The "&" of a beat is the second half of the beat, as when counting eighth notes: 1 & 2 & 3 & 4 &.

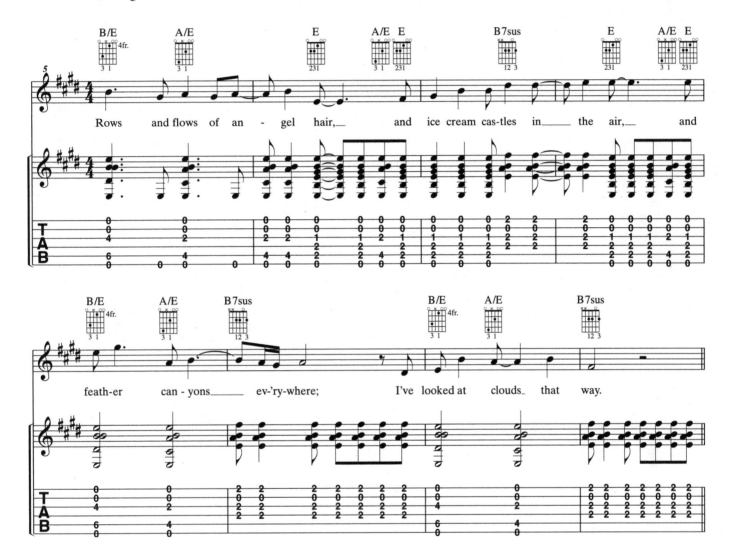

BOTH SIDES NOW

Capo at 2nd fret to match original recording.

Moderately slow

Words and Music by
JONI MITCHELL

1. Rows and flows of an-gel hair,__ and ice cream cas-tles in__ the air,__ and

2.3. *See additional lyrics*

feath-er can-yons__ ev-'ry-where; I've looked at clouds__ that

way. But now they on-ly block the sun;__ they

rain and snow__ on ev-'ry-one.__ So man-y things I__

__ would have done, but clouds got in my way. I've

*Original recording in F♯ major.

**Sung octave lower.

Both Sides Now - 2 - 1

Verse 2:
Moons and Junes and Ferris wheels,
The dizzy dancing way you feel,
As ev'ry fairy tale comes real;
I've looked at love that way.
But now it's just another show;
You leave 'em laughing when you go.
And if you care, don't let them know;
Don't give yourself away.

Chorus 2:
I've looked at love from both sides now,
From give and take, and still somehow
It's love's illusions I recall.
I really don't know love at all.

Verse 3:
Tears and fears and feeling proud,
To say "I love you" right out loud,
Dreams and schemes and circus crowds;
I've looked at life that way.
But now old friends are acting strange;
They shake their heads, they say I've changed.
Well, something's lost but something's gained
In living every day.

Chorus 3:
I've looked at life from both sides now,
From win and lose, and still somehow
It's life's illusions I recall.
I really don't know life at all.

Can't Find My Way Home

Key Thoughts

"I'm wasted and I can't find my way home." Does any lyric sum up the '60s experience more succinctly? Blind Faith was a band born out of the innocence and optimism of youth only to confront the harsh realities of the world. The super group's short-lived career lasted only one album and a single tour.

Take Note

The key to playing this tune is feeling at home with a simple fingerpicking pattern that repeats throughout. In fingerpicking notation, letters denote the right-hand fingers. (This is assuming you're a right-handed guitar player; otherwise the reverse is true.)

p = thumb
i = index finger
m = middle finger
a = ring finger

In the example below, you'll only use your thumb *p*, index finger *i*, and middle finger *m*. Repeat the pattern until it's learned into your hand's muscle memory and you can play it without any thought.

We've transcribed a couple of Eric Clapton's melodic interludes and included them in this arrangement. Have some fun picking them out as you listen to the recording.

🌸 Fun Fact

The 1969 release of Blind Faith's self-titled (and only) album immediately ran into controversy with its provocative, perhaps scandalous, cover image, which featured photographer Bob Seidermann's shot of a topless 11-year-old girl holding a silver spaceship. Ironically, the title of the photograph was "Blind Faith," a phrase that so perfectly underscored Eric Clapton's outlook on the new project that he adopted it as the band's name. The cover of the U.S. release of the album, however, was changed to feature a shot of the band instead.

CAN'T FIND MY WAY HOME

Words and Music by
STEVE WINWOOD

Can't Find My Way Home - 5 - 1

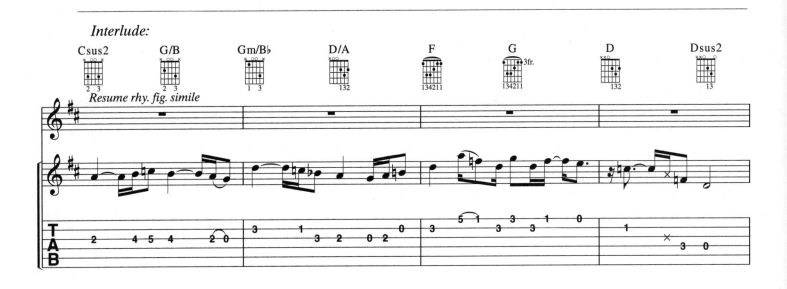

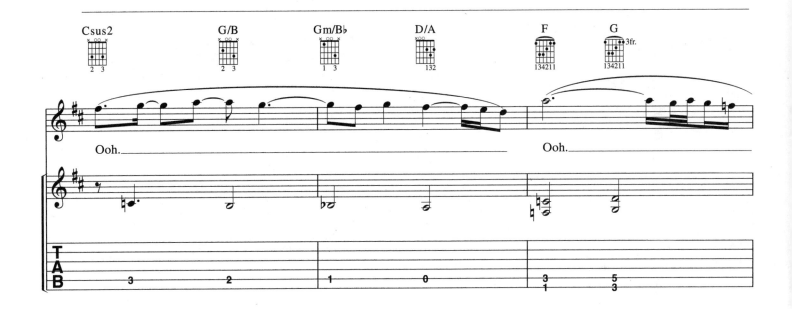

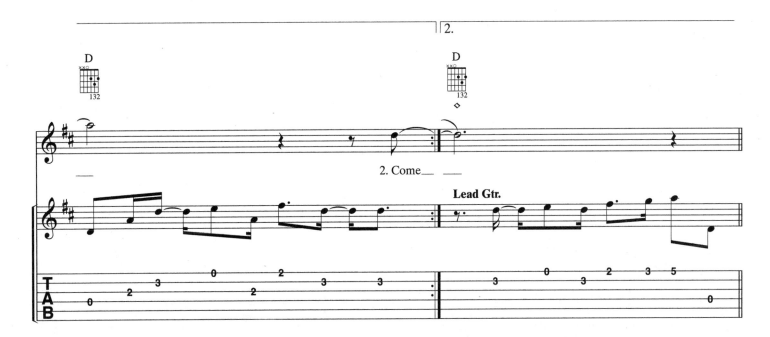

Ooh,_____ but I can't find_ my_ way_ home._____

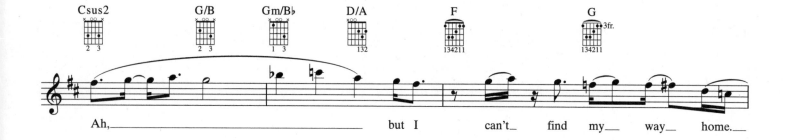

Ah,_____ but I can't_ find my_ way_ home.___

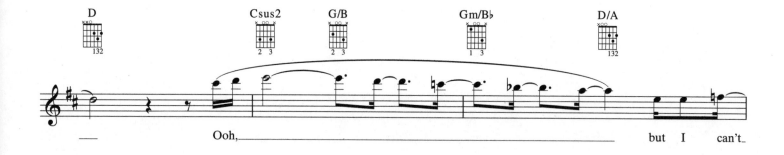

___ Ooh,_____ but I can't_

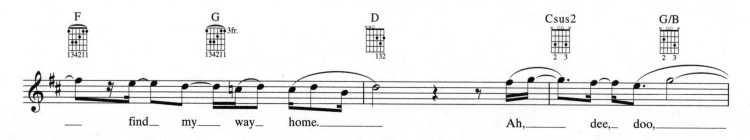

___ find_ my_ way_ home._____ Ah,_____ dee,_ doo,_____

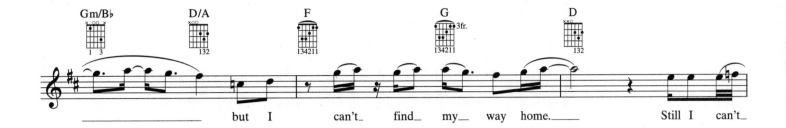

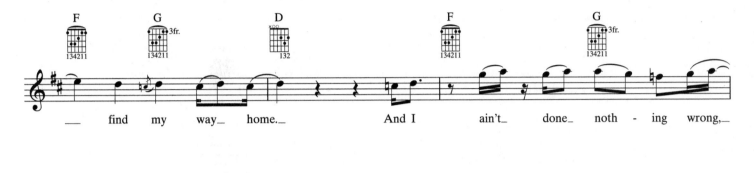

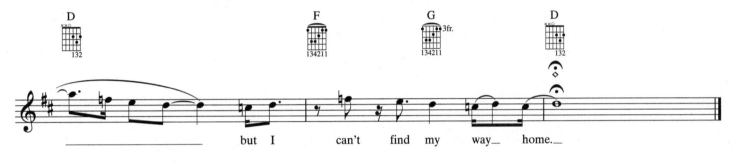

Verse 2:
Come down on your own and leave your body alone.
Somebody must change.
You are the reason I've been waiting all these years.
Somebody holds the key.

Chorus 2:
Well, I'm near the end, I just ain't got the time,
Oh, and I'm wasted and I can't find my way home.

Can't Find My Way Home - 5 - 5

Cat's in the Cradle

Key Thoughts

"Cat's in the Cradle" was Harry Chapin's most commercially successful song, reaching No. 1 on the pop charts in December of 1974—not a bad achievement for a man whose ambitions did not originally lie in songwriting. The lyrics were derived from a poem penned by his wife, Sandy, and tell the poignant tale of a father so consumed with work that he finds no time for his son. Eventually, the son grows up and is unwilling to make time for his father, turning the tables on the old man who realizes too late, "My boy was just like me."

Take Note

The original recording of "Cat's in the Cradle" employs a capo on the eighth fret. The fingerpicking pattern on the intro and first three verses includes an alternating bass played with the thumb in a style commonly known as Travis picking. (For a detailed explanation of the Travis picking technique, see the notes for the song "Never Going Back Again.") Use your thumb to keep a steady pulse on all of the down-stem notes, and once you're comfortable with that, begin introducing the notes with up-stems.

Notice that a basic strum pattern of quarter-note down-strokes is introduced on the chorus. Fingerpicking resumes on the second and third verses, but from the third chorus to the end, everything is strummed.

Guitar Gods

Singer-songwriter **HARRY CHAPIN** was an artist with many talents. While in high school, he formed a band and sang in a boys' choir, but it was actually a career in documentary filmmaking, not music, that he pursued in college. He found almost immediate success when a film he directed, *Legendary Champions*, received a nomination for an Academy Award.

The music world was fortunate, though, when Chapin decided to switch careers a few years later. His first foray into music came in the summer of 1972 with the release of his debut album, *Heads and Tails*. It included the hit song "Taxi," which soon became one of his signature tunes. Chapin's most successful album, *Verities and Balderdash*, was released two years later. Featuring his biggest hit song, "Cat's in the Cradle," the album peaked at No. 4 on the U.S. charts and went on to become a gold record. Shortly after its release, Chapin branched off into further artistic exploration and began working on a musical, *The Night That Made America Famous*, which earned two Tony nominations. Tragically, the life of this diverse and beloved artist was cut short by an auto accident in 1981.

CAT'S IN THE CRADLE

Capo 8th fret to match recording.

Words and Music by
HARRY CHAPIN and SANDY CHAPIN

Moderately, with a 2 feel

1. My

Verses 1-3:

child   ar - rived__   just   the   oth - er   day,   he   came   to   the   world,   in   the
son   turned__   ten   just   the   oth - er   day,   he   said,   "Thanks   for   the   ball,   Dad,   come
came   from   col - lege   just   the   oth - er   day,   so   much   like   a   man,   I   just

Cat's in the Cradle - 5 - 1

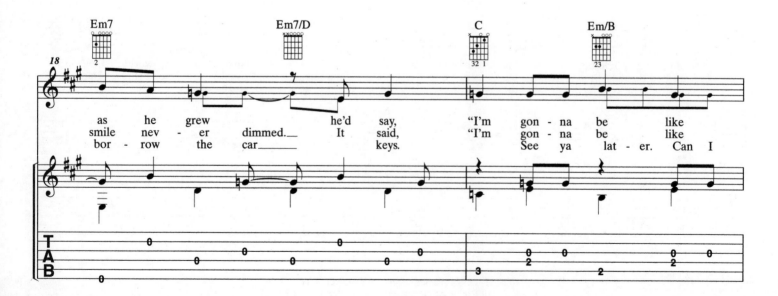

Classical Gas

Key Thoughts

"Classical Gas" introduced many people to the beauty and power of instrumental guitar music. The song is an impressive tour de force that wows friends and family—but the good news is that it sounds much harder than it really is. Like many great guitar pieces, "Classical Gas" lies very naturally on the instrument. It's also a great piece for learning to fingerpick properly, beyond just simple accompaniment patterns.

Take Note

This arrangement is simplified, but pretty close to the original recorded version. It is played fingerstyle. Use your thumb to play the down-stem notes (the bass lines) and your fingers to play the up-stem notes (the melody). It will help to "plant" your index, middle, and ring fingers on the top three strings; generally, those three fingers will play the notes on those strings while your thumb plays the notes on the bottom three strings.

The seven-measure intro contains the famous melody, which is played slowly and without a strong rhythmic pulse. Playing within chord shapes is the key to making this flow like the recording, so always hold the indicated shape through each measure and pick out the correct notes.

One of the most identifiable and exciting aspects of this song is that it has many interesting rhythmic changes. For example, look at the $\frac{6}{4}$ bar in the second line of music on the second page. This series of arpeggios creates an interesting tension by accenting groups of three notes instead of groups of two. It's easy to play, though, because all you really have to do is hold the indicated chord shapes and pick a constant stream of eighth notes.

Guitar Gods

MASON WILLIAMS was already an Emmy Award-winning comedy writer for the *Smothers Brothers Comedy Hour* when he broke out as a virtuosic guitar artist in the 1960s. Warner Bros. Records was looking to add 10 new artists at the time, and Tom Smothers suggested the label give Williams a chance. He released his first effort in 1968, *The Mason Williams Phonograph Record*, which peaked at No. 14 and won two Grammy Awards for the chart-topping hit "Classical Gas."

CLASSICAL GAS

By MASON WILLIAMS

Moderately

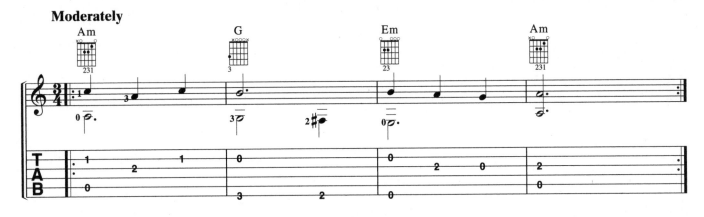

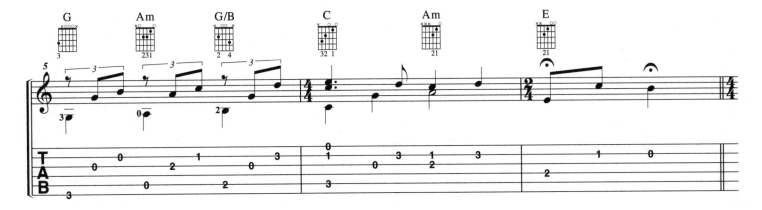

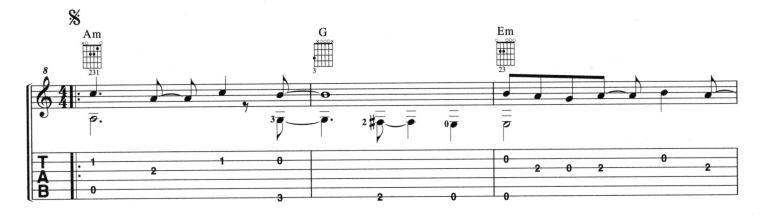

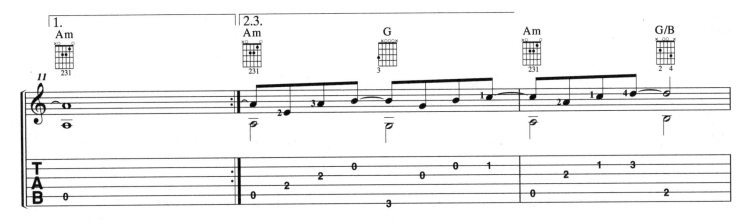

Classical Gas - 5 - 1

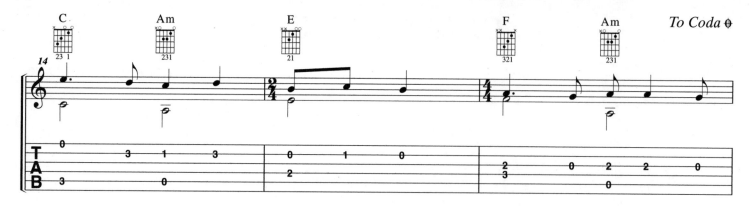

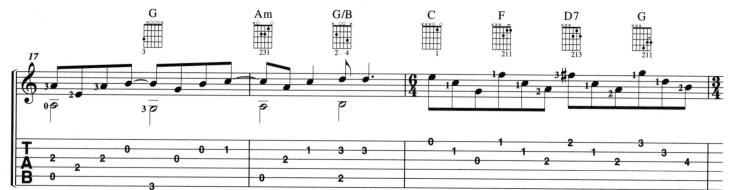

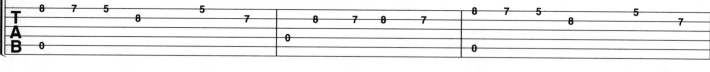

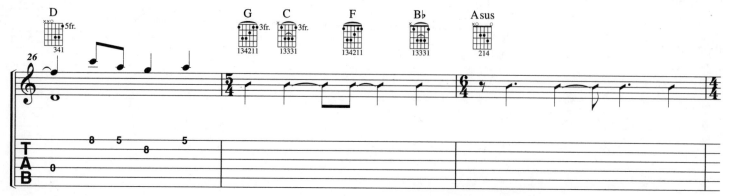

Classical Gas - 5 - 2

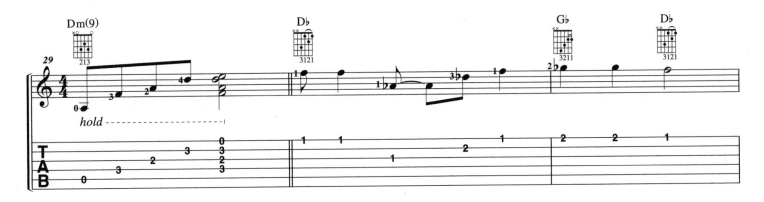

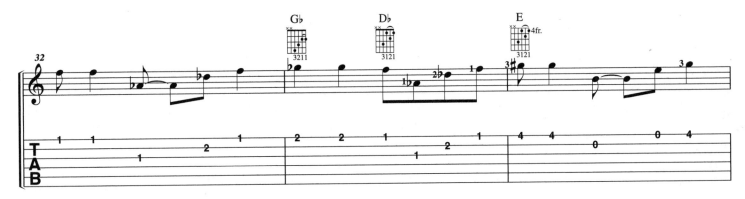

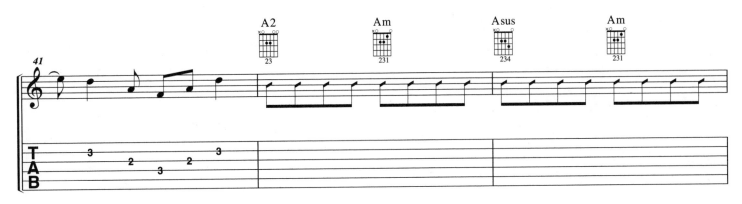

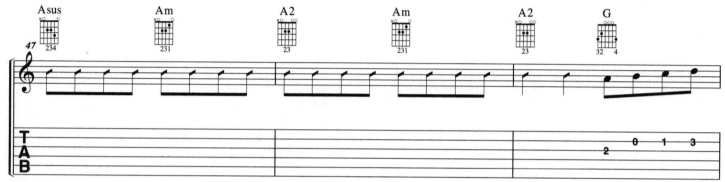

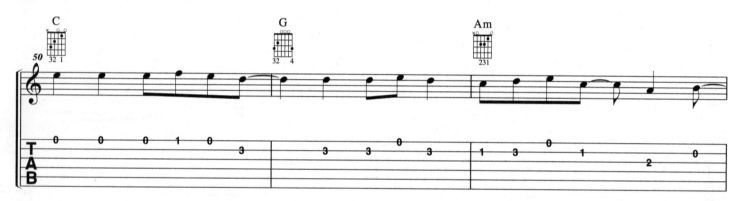

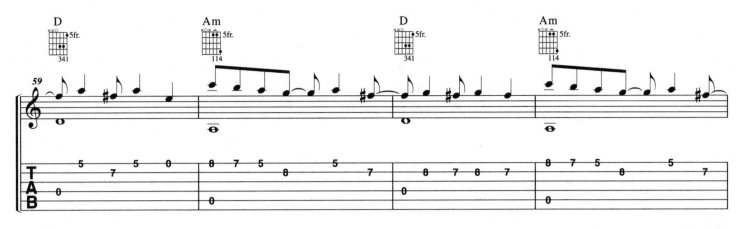

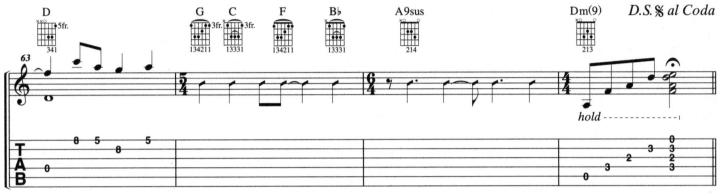

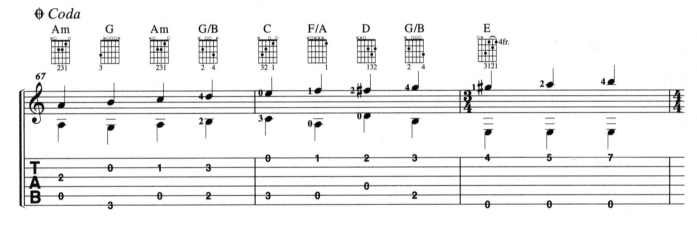

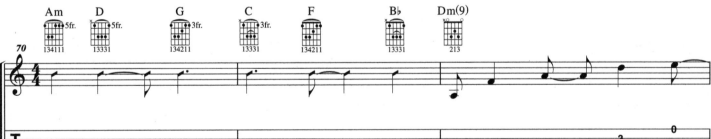

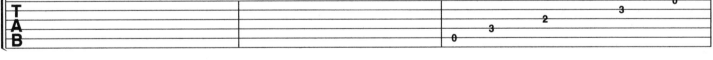

Copperline

"Copperline" opens with one of the simplest and most common of all chord progressions, but James Taylor put his own stamp on it and created a thing of unique beauty. Although this part sounds simple, it can be a surprising challenge to play because of James's special fingering—but don't worry, we'll also show you a simplified version of the pattern.

The intro guitar part, which also forms the backbone to most of the verses, is just D to Bm7, but with a very unique fingering for the D chord. Before tackling the authentic version, try the simplified pattern in the first example below. Here are a couple of things to keep in mind:

- ◆ For the D chord, be sure to use your 2nd, 3rd, and 1st fingers on strings 3, 2, and 1 as shown in the chord frame. Then, your 1st finger will continually shift between the 1st string for the D chord and the 5th string for the Bm7 chord.

- ◆ This pattern actually implies two separate parts at the same time: an alternating bass and a strummed guitar. This type of hybrid fingerpicking/strumming pattern is something James is very good at. Use your thumb to play the bass notes (stems down), then strum the D chord in an alternating motion with your index finger. The arrows indicate the index finger's down-strums and up-strums, also called *brush strokes*. Example 1A is the basic pattern, and 1B is a variation.

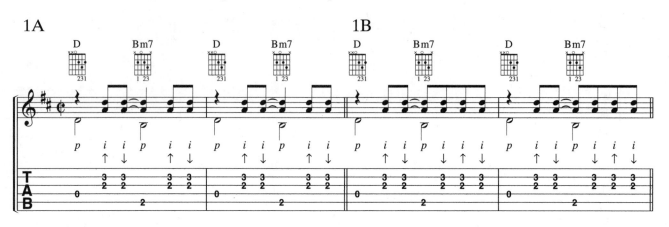

 Tip

To keep the 1st string from sounding as you play the pattern, your index finger should strum through the 3rd and 2nd strings and then briefly come to rest on the 1st string without pushing through it.

The next example is the complete intro figure, exactly as James plays it. The main difference is the addition of a little melody on the 1st string, giving the illusion of three simultaneous guitar parts: bass line, strum, and melody. Assuming you can play the simplified pattern with no problem, all you have to do to add the 1st-string melody is "catch" the E and F♯ notes with the up-strum of your index finger.

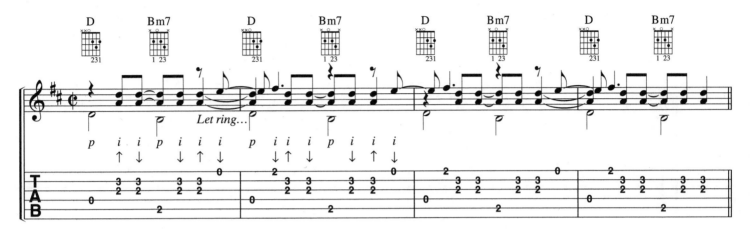

There are many interesting chord progressions in the song that are basically just the D chord with a moving bass line. A good example of this is in bars 15 and 16 of the verse, which is shown below.

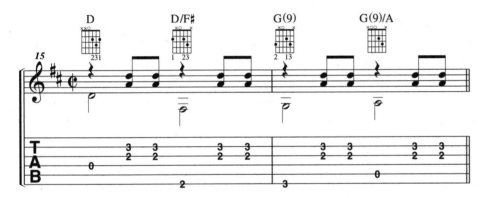

The rest of the song is pretty simple. For the chorus, you can just strum half-note chords as indicated. During the interlude, the melody is sung over sustained whole-note chords; this is very easy, but also beautiful due to the unique Gmaj9 chord. You can see that the Gmaj9 looks exactly like a D chord with a G in the bass.

🎼 Tip

To match the record key, you'll need to capo your guitar at the second fret. Some people think that using a capo is like cheating—just an excuse for not learning chords in every key. But that's not true at all. Using a capo allows us to take advantage of all the natural beauty of open strings and interesting guitar chords in any key.

Guitar Gods

Known for his timeless acoustic guitar tunes, singer/songwriter **JAMES TAYLOR** got his big start in 1968 when he signed with the Beatles's Apple Records label. His lengthy career spans four decades and a marriage to Carly Simon. His best-selling album, *Greatest Hits*, received diamond certification in 2000, totaling more than 10 million copies sold to date.

COPPERLINE

Words and Music by
JAMES TAYLOR and
REYNOLDS PRICE

Capo at 2nd fret to match original recording.

Copperline - 4 - 1

Her - cu - les and a hog - nosed snake,
Sour mash and new moon - shine,

down on Cop - per - line,

we were down on Cop - per - line.

Day breaks_ and the boy wakes up and the dog barks_ and the bird sings_ and the

sap ris - es and the an - gels sigh,_ yeah._

Interlude:
Gmaj9

G(9)/A   *D.S. % al Coda*

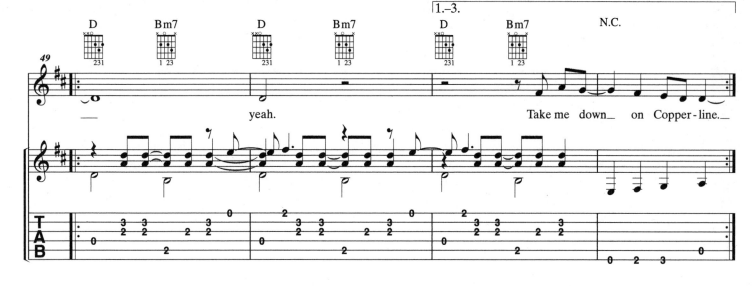

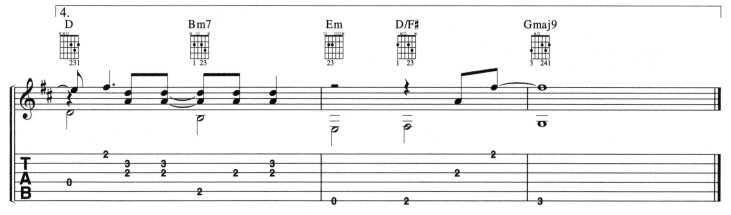

Verse 3:
The first kiss ever I took,
Like a page from a romance book.
The sky opened and the earth shook,
Down on Copperline,
Down on Copperline.
(To Instrumental:)

Chorus 3:
Took a fall from a windy height,
I only knew how to hold on tight,
And pray for love enough to last all night,
Down on Copperline.
(To Interlude:)

Verse 4:
I tried to go back, as if I could
All spec house and plywood.
Tore up and tore up good,
Down on Copperline.
It doesn't come as a surprise to me,
It doesn't touch my memory.
Man, I'm lifting up and rising free,
Down over Copperline.
(To Chorus 4:)

Chorus 4:
Half a mile down to Morgan Creek,
Leaning heavy on the end of the week.
Hercules and a hog-nosed snake,
Down on Copperline,
We were down on Copperline.
Down on Copperline,
We were down on Copperline.

Danny's Song

Key Thoughts

"Danny's Song" is a solo feature that Kenny Loggins performed with Loggins & Messina. The basic fingerpicking accompaniment is a simplified Travis picking pattern, and learning this song is great preparation for playing songs with more complex Travis patterns. For a definition of Travis picking and another great song example, see Lindsey Buckingham's "Never Going Back Again," later in this book.

Take Note

The first thing to work on is understanding the correct rhythmic *groove*, or feel. Without the right groove, the song just won't feel right. Notice the time signature at the beginning of the first measure; it's a "C" with a slash through it ₵. This symbol means *cut time*. Cut time is $\frac{2}{2}$: 2 beats per measure, and a half note gets one beat. To get into this feel, tap your foot at a medium tempo *two* times per measure, not four. That means each grouping of four eighth notes is played in the space of one foot tap. Now place a slight accent (stress) on the last note of each four-note group, allowing that note to ring out a little bit more than the others. Once you do that, the accent patterns will automatically change, and you'll be grooving right.

Now we're ready to work on the fingerpicking pattern. Most Travis patterns are more complex than the one in this song, and our version is even slightly simplified from how Kenny Loggins actually performs it. To play this pattern, your thumb needs to constantly alternate between two strings on each quarter-note beat. The thumb notes are indicated with down-stems in the notation. In between the thumb strokes, just alternate using your index and middle fingers. Try the D chord pattern shown below.

🌸 Fun Fact

Jim Messina, a very experienced guitarist and producer, was originally hired to produce the first record by a very young Kenny Loggins. The pairing was so successful, however, that the record label asked them to tour and perform as a duo—and Loggins & Messina was born.

We have two important fingerings to point out. First, when transitioning from the D chord to the C(9), keep your 3rd finger locked on the 2nd-string D at the third fret. That will be your pivot point. Since that note is common to both chords, continue to hold it while your other fingers move to play the C(9) chord.

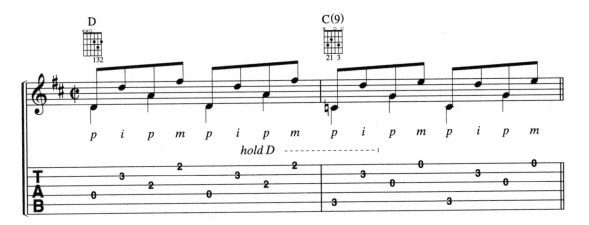

The other fingering is on the A chord in measures 7 and 8. Look at the example below, and you'll see that a little melody is created by changing the last note of each four-note group. The melody is C#–D–E. To play this, hold the A chord, then slide your 3rd finger up to D at the end of the first measure and keep it there. The E is the open 1st string, so you can continue holding your 3rd finger on D through bar 8 and again use it as a pivot point to transition back to the D chord in measure 9.

DANNY'S SONG

Words and Music by
KENNY LOGGINS

Danny's Song - 2 - 1

Verse 3:
Pisces, Virgo rising is a very good sign,
Strong and kind,
And the little boy is mine.
Now I see a family where there once was none.
Now we've just begun,
Yeah, we're going to fly to the sun.
(To Chorus:)

Verse 4:
Love the girl who holds the world in a paper cup.
Drink it up,
Love her and she'll bring you luck.
And if you find she helps your mind, buddy, take her home,
Don't you live alone, try to earn what lovers own.
(To Chorus:)

Early Mornin' Rain

Key Thoughts

Written in 1964, "Early Mornin' Rain" was one of Gordon Lightfoot's first recorded compositions. Bob Dylan released a notable cover of the song on his *Self Portrait* album in 1970, and this plaintive tale of a lonely man far from home has subsequently been recorded by artists ranging from Elvis Presley to Paul Weller.

Take Note

The guitar accompaniment throughout "Early Mornin' Rain" is a fairly rapid strumming pattern: down, down, down-up-down-up. Keep your strumming wrist relaxed and loose or you'll never make it to the fourth verse.

Note the tempo sign, "Moderately fast in 2." The term "in 2" applies to cut time, because there are two strong pulses in each measure. (See the explanation of cut time in the lesson for "Danny's Song.")

There are just three chords in this song, and they're all open, first-position chords—no barre chords. That makes it a good song for practicing speed during chord transitions. When changing from one chord to the next, always keep in mind the concept of *economy of motion*, and move your fingers as little as possible. Learn not to lift your fingers too far off the fretboard, and you'll be switching chords quickly in no time.

Tip

Economy of motion is the key to smooth and easy guitar playing. Be as direct as possible when moving to a new note or chord, and lift only as far off the fretboard as necessary.

Guitar Gods

Canadian singer/songwriter **GORDON LIGHTFOOT** first gained recognition as a songwriter in the mid-1960s when the popular folk group Peter, Paul, and Mary performed his song "Early Mornin' Rain" on their 1965 release *See What Tomorrow Brings*. The song peaked at No. 11 on the charts. In 1966, Lightfoot released his debut recording, *Lightfoot*, and critics raved at the unusually mature songwriting. The album included his version of "Early Mornin' Rain," along with the classics "The Way I Feel" and "Ribbon of Darkness."

EARLY MORNIN' RAIN

Capo 3rd fret to match recording.

Words and Music by
GORDON LIGHTFOOT

Moderately fast in 2

Verse 3:
Hear the mighty engines roar,
See the silver bird on high;
She's away and westward bound.
Far above the clouds she'll fly,
Where the mornin' rain don't fall
And the sun always shines.
She'll be flying o'er my home
In about three hours time.

Verse 4:
This old airport's got me down;
It's no earthly good to me.
And I'm stuck here on the ground,
As cold and drunk as I can be.
You can't jump a jet plane
Like you can a freight train;
So, I'd best be on my way
In the early mornin' rain.

Early Mornin' Rain - 3 - 3

Friend of the Devil

Grateful Dead's "Friend of the Devil" tells the tale of an outlaw on the run from both the law and Old Scratch. The acoustic arrangement and double-time tempo highlight the Dead's bluegrass roots.

The basic riff in "Friend of the Devil" is a descending G major scale picked under a G chord and then a C chord. As you play it, keep your fingers anchored in the chord position as much as possible. Start with a down-pick on the 3rd-string G and follow it with a quick down-up on the upper strings of the G chord. Keep your 3rd finger fixed on the 1st string as you continue alternating between the scale notes and the down-up strums on the G chord. Keep holding the G chord until you change to the C chord, then keep your fingers anchored in the C chord position as much as the descending bass line permits.

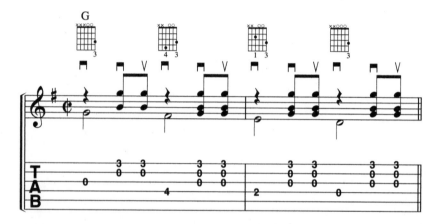

At the D chord in bar 14, the guitar part switches to a straight alternating bass rhythm that is very characteristic of bluegrass music. The typical alternating bass goes back and forth between the root and the 5th of the chord, and here the alternating notes are on the 4th and 5th strings.

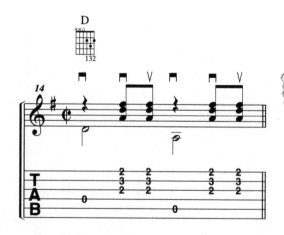

Fun Fact

Despite their studio successes, Grateful Dead kept their focus on being primarily a live act. Tours were lengthened, shows added, and the mass of loyal fans who followed the band in their tie-dyed clothes and VW Microbuses soon became known as "Deadheads."

FRIEND OF THE DEVIL

Words by
ROBERT HUNTER

Music by
JERRY GARCIA and
JOHN DAWSON

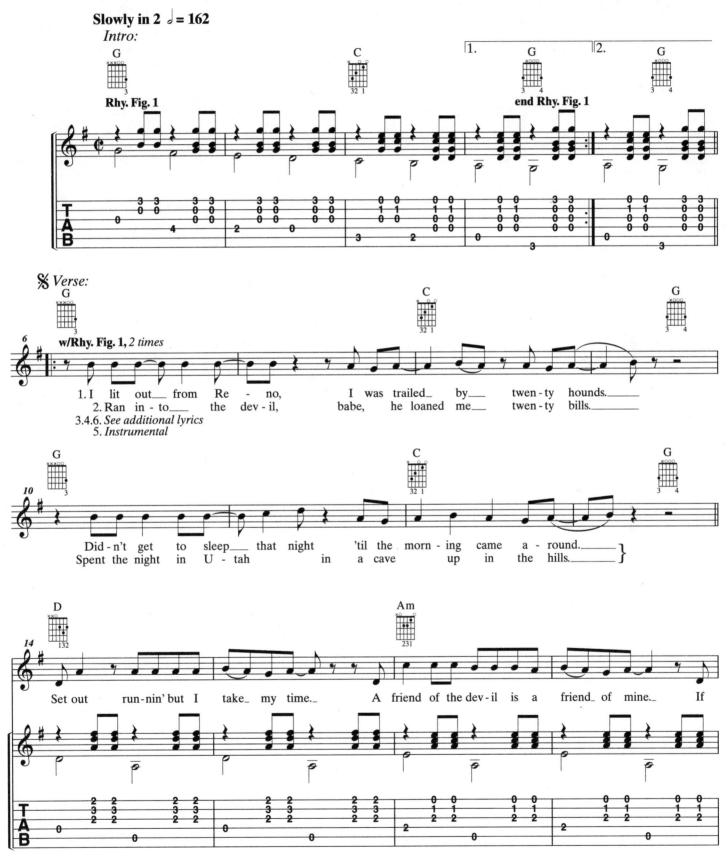

Friend of the Devil - 3 - 1

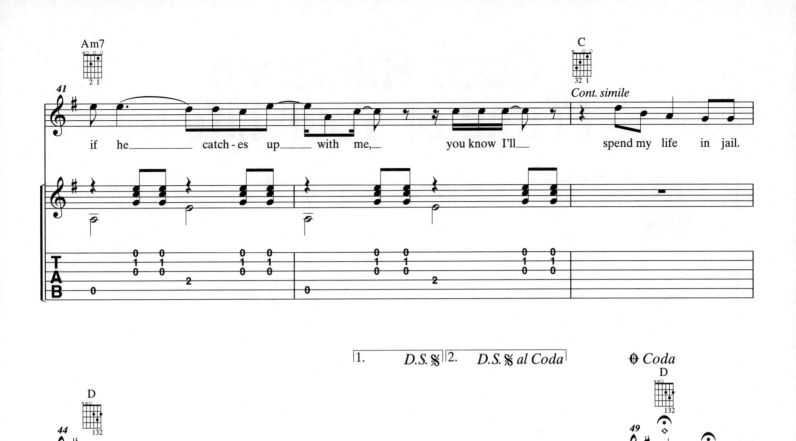

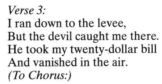

Verse 3:
I ran down to the levee,
But the devil caught me there.
He took my twenty-dollar bill
And vanished in the air.
(To Chorus:)

Verses 4 & 6:
Got a wife in Chino, babe,
And one in Cherokee.
The first one says she's got my child,
But it don't look like me.
(To Chorus:)

Good Riddance (Time of Your Life)

Key Thoughts

American punk band Green Day struck a mellow, reflective pose with "Good Riddance (Time of Your Life)." Released in the period between the band's 1994 breakout success and their 2004 rise to mega-superstar status with *American Idiot*, this introspective acoustic ballad (with strings!) was an about-face for a band heretofore known for edgy, hard-driving rock.

Take Note

Billie Joe Armstrong plays the guitar on "Good Riddance" in a casual, arpeggiated fashion. Note that, while holding the G5 chord position, the left-hand 2nd finger extends up to the third fret of the 6th string, muting the 5th string in the process. Strum down with a pick, emphasizing the bass strings, then repeat the down-strum and quickly follow it with an up-stroke across the 2nd and 3rd strings together. Next, individually pick open strings 3, 4, and 3 using up-stroke, down-stroke, up-stroke (respectively), and you've got the basic arpeggio pattern of the introduction, first verse, and chorus. Try it slowly at first, and gradually build up speed until you can play along with the recording without a second thought.

𝄞 Tip

See how the 3rd finger remains stationary on the third fret of the 2nd string for the first three chords (G5, Csus2, D5)? Don't move that finger. Keep it planted firmly in place, and try to minimize the movement of your fingers at all times. As a general rule, when two sequential chords share a note, try not to remove that finger from the fretboard as you transition from one chord to the next; you'll be able to make the chord changes more smoothly and quickly that way.

From measure 27 in the chorus to the 3rd ending, you have the option of strumming the chords, arpeggiating each chord throughout, or breaking the monotony and giving the performance more dynamic interest by picking one part and strumming rhythm on another. When strumming, use the pattern below. Notice that full chords are used here, not the "5" and sus2 chords employed in the arpegiatted introduction. Similar to the picked pattern at the beginning, you should emphasize the bass strings of each chord with a down-stroke on beat 1 of each measure. Note the *accent* > on beat 2, which tells you to strum all the notes of the chord with more force on that beat.

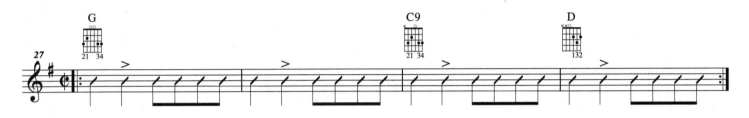

To finish, resume the intro arpeggios for a return to a softer style at the 3rd ending.

Fun Fact

"Good Riddance (Time of Your Life)" was featured over a retrospective montage on the final episode of *Seinfeld* in 1998.

GOOD RIDDANCE (TIME OF YOUR LIFE)

Lyrics by BILLIE JOE
Music by BILLIE JOE and GREEN DAY

A Horse with No Name

Key Thoughts

Originally titled "Desert Song," Dewey Bunnell's song was inspired by the arid environment surrounding Vandenburg Air Force Base where he spent part of his childhood. An imaginary traveler describes the sights and sounds of the desert while riding a "horse with no name," expressing how the natural setting can be used as a refuge from the stresses of everyday life. In the final verse, he calls attention to the need for preserving nature and the environment.

Take Note

"A Horse with No Name" is a poster child for minimalist composition. The whole song uses only two chords (Em and D6/9), and almost the entire melody steps between just two notes.

The basic strum pattern includes *accents* > in the rhythm. Emphasize the beats with the accents, but once you're comfortable with the basic pattern, feel free to vary the pattern and inject accents in other places, too.

The guitar solo in this transcription includes some rapid triplet picking. When playing these figures, your pick hand should use a constant alternating up-and-down motion.

Definition

An **accent** means to stress a note or chord by playing it slightly louder.

Guitar Gods

The group **AMERICA** was actually formed in London by the sons of U.S. Air Force officers stationed in Great Britain. The band's first single, "A Horse with No Name" reached No. 3 when it hit English stores in 1971, and flew to the top of the charts in the United States after the band's coming to the states. Most listeners mistook this breakout recording by America as a Neil Young song; ironically, it displaced Young's "Heart of Gold" from the No. 1 slot in 1972.

A HORSE WITH NO NAME

Words and Music by
DEWEY BUNNELL

A Horse With No Name - 3 - 1

Verse 2:
After two days in the desert sun
My skin began to turn red.
After three days in the desert fun
I was looking at a river bed.
And the story it told of a river that flowed
Made me sad to think it was dead.
You see, I've…
(To Chorus:)

Verse 3:
After nine days I let the horse run free
'Cause the desert had turned to sea.
There were plants and birds and rocks and things,
There were sand and hills and rings.
The ocean is a desert with its life underground
And the perfect disguise above.
Under the cities lies a heart made of ground,
But the humans will give no love.
You see, I've…
(To Chorus:)

I'll Have to Say I Love You in a Song

Key Thoughts

"I'll Have to Say I Love You in a Song" is a classic ballad from Jim Croce. He uses several of his most characteristic writing tools in this song, such as major 7th chords and the occasional "surprise" chord to grab your attention (in this case, G#7).

Take Note

As with all of Jim Croce's great ballads, the original recording features two interwoven guitar parts. If you listen to the recording with a set of headphones, you'll hear Jim's lower guitar on the left and Maury Muehleisen's higher guitar harmony on the right. Our arrangement presents a slightly simplified version of Jim's part.

You might find the intro guitar part just a little challenging at first. Use your thumb to play the bass notes, which are all indicated with down-stems. The rhythm created by this thumb pattern is relatively common, but very interesting, and pretty much defines the feel of the guitar part. Think of each measure as a group of eight eighth notes. The typical subdivision would create four equally strong beats felt as **1** & **2** & **3** & **4** &, but this thumb pattern breaks the measure into two groups of three eighth notes plus one group of two eighth notes, which is felt as **1** 2 3 **1** 2 3 **1** 2. If you count it that way quickly and tap your foot on "1" each time, you'll feel the basic rhythm to this guitar part.

In many guitar songs, the guitar part of the intro is essentially the same as what is played for the verse. In this song, the verse figure is just a little simpler than the intro. Below is our suggestion for how to play through this part. On the E chord, we've incorporated a little moving bass line that Jim performs, but you can simply play the basic fingerpicking pattern throughout the E chord if you prefer.

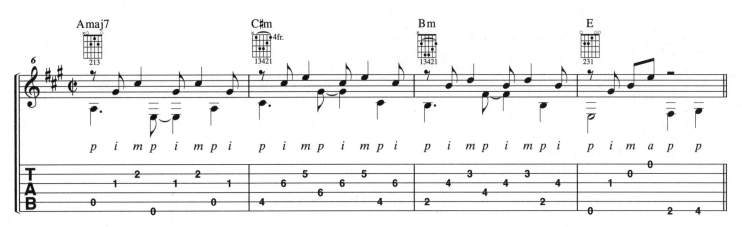

Guitar Gods

JIM CROCE's right-hand man and musical partner was his guitarist, Maury Muehleisen. Muehleisen's tasteful playing provided the perfect complement to Croce's poignant style. What many don't know is that Muehleisen was a singer/songwriter as well. Croce and Muehleisen met while playing in the same coffeehouses in the late '60s and immediately formed a musical bond.

Ironically, it was Croce who played backup in the beginning. When Muehleisen got a recording contract from Capitol Records, he invited Croce to play with him. Muehleisen's debut, *Gingerbread*, was released in 1970 but failed to make much of an impression. The two continued to play together until Croce himself got a recording contract. Returning the favor, Croce invited Muehleisen to play on his debut. This marked the beginning of a succession of acclaimed Jim Croce albums that featured Maury Muehleisen's exquisite guitar playing. Tragically, Muehleisen died in the same plane crash that claimed Croce's life.

I'LL HAVE TO SAY I LOVE YOU IN A SONG

Words and Music by
JIM CROCE

I'll Have to Say I Love You in a Song - 2 - 1

Verse 4:
Yeah, I know it's kind of late,
I hope I didn't wake you,
But there's something that I just gotta say,
I knew you'd understand.
'Cause every time I tried to tell you,
The words just came out wrong,
So I'll have to say I love you in a song.

If You Could Read My Mind

Key Thoughts

Ontario-born Gordon Lightfoot performed on the folk circuit for over 10 years before becoming an "overnight" success with the gentle ballad "If You Could Read My Mind" in 1971.

Take Note

The guitar accompaniment for "If You Could Read My Mind" is a fairly simple finger-picking pattern that repeats throughout the song. The thumb plays the bass note of each chord, which means it plays the 6th string for G, the 5th string for C, and the 4th string for D. The other fingers arpeggiate the chords and should remain fixed to their assigned strings: the index finger plays the 4th string, the middle finger plays the 3rd string, and the ring finger plays the 2nd string.

Guitar Gods

GORDON LIGHTFOOT's 1970 single "If You Could Read My Mind," from the poor-selling album *Sit Down Stranger,* became such a big hit that his record company decided to capitalize on the success and renamed the album in 1971 to *If You Could Read My Mind.* The record featured guitarist Red Shea and bassist Rick Haynes, who were Gordon's usual backing musicians of the time, but also received help from some of the best on the Warner/Reprise label. The all-star band included Ry Cooder (bottleneck guitar and mandolin), John Sebastian (autoharp, harmonica, and electric guitar), and Van Dyke Parks (harmonium). Randy Newman even worked on string arrangements for two tracks. Throughout the 1970s, Lightfoot released one classic after another. His 1974 album *Sundown,* with its hit title track, went to No. 1 on the U.S. charts. Other hits of the era include "Carefree Highway," "The Circle Is Small (I Can See It in Your Eyes)," and "The Wreck of the Edmund Fitzgerald," which was an unexpected hit given that its lyrics were taken directly from a *Newsweek* article about the sinking of the ship during a severe storm. Despite the decline in popularity of folk music over the time of his lengthy career, Gordon Lightfoot continues to record and in 2004 released his 20th album, *Harmony.*

IF YOU COULD READ MY MIND

Words and Music by
GORDON LIGHTFOOT

Capo 2nd fret to match recording.

Moderately

If You Could Read My Mind - 5 - 1

long as I'm a ghost___ that you can't see.___
cause the end - ing's just___ too hard to take.___

Cont. rhy. simile

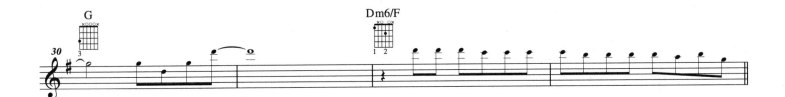

Bridge:

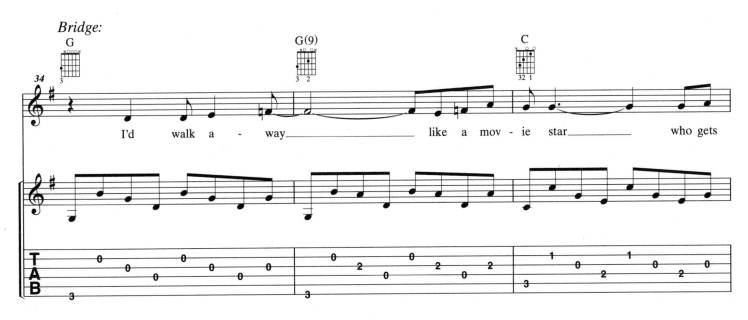

I'd walk a - way_____ like a mov - ie star_____ who gets

Layla (Unplugged)

Key Thoughts

In 1992, Eric Clapton completely reinvented his signature song "Layla" for his *MTV Unplugged* special. Performed on acoustic guitars with a lazy shuffle feel and without the original driving signature riff, this version was so different from the original that Clapton asked the audience, "See if you can spot this one."

Take Note

The song has an underlying *shuffle* feel, meaning the eighth notes are played long-short instead of exactly even. Listen carefully to the recording and imitate the feel.

The main acoustic guitar part is a two-bar pattern. It's right up front in the intro, repeated on each chorus, and can be played throughout the guitar solo section. Follow the left hand fingerings as shown below in the notation and chord frames.

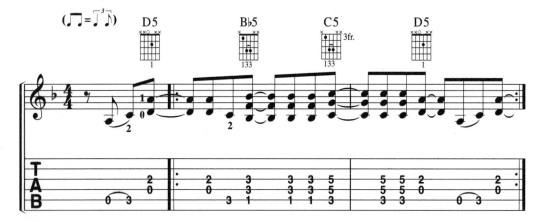

If you want to try improvising a guitar solo, work with the D minor pentatonic scale as shown in the figure below, which spans three positions on the neck of the guitar. Try improvising melodies both vertically (across the strings) and horizontally (up and down single strings).

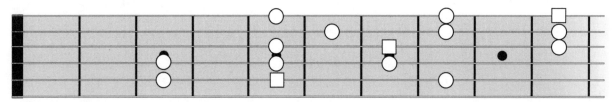

The D minor pentatonic scale.

Guitar Gods

Though internationally revered as one of the greatest guitarists of his generation, **ERIC CLAPTON** was surprisingly reluctant to break out as a solo artist. In 1970, his self-titled solo debut album peaked at No. 13, but before the record even hit store shelves, he'd taken himself out of the spotlight to form Derek & the Dominos. Four years and a kicked drug addiction later, Clapton made his permanent return as a solo artist with *461 Ocean Boulevard*, reaching No. 1.

LAYLA
(Unplugged)

Words and Music by
ERIC CLAPTON and JIM GORDON

Moderately ♩ = 96

Intro:

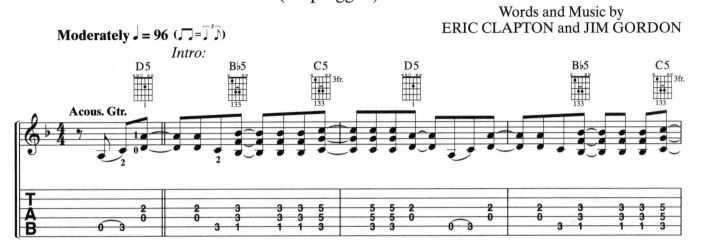

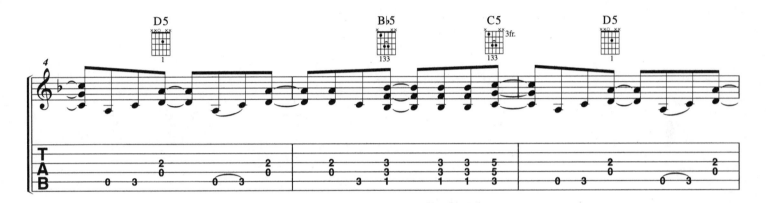

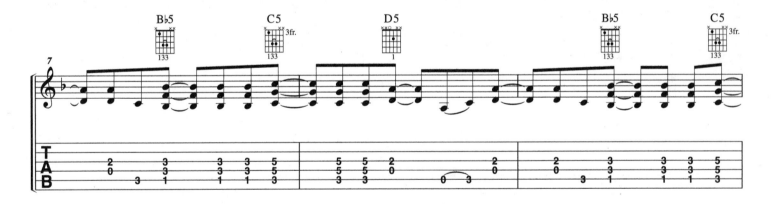

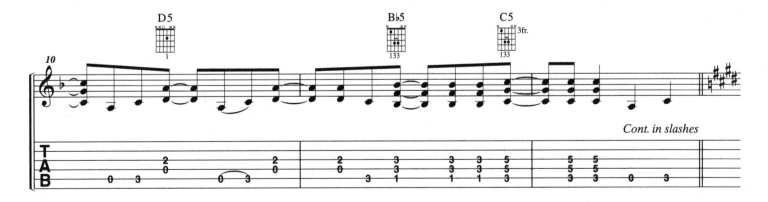

Cont. in slashes

Layla (Unplugged) - 3 - 1

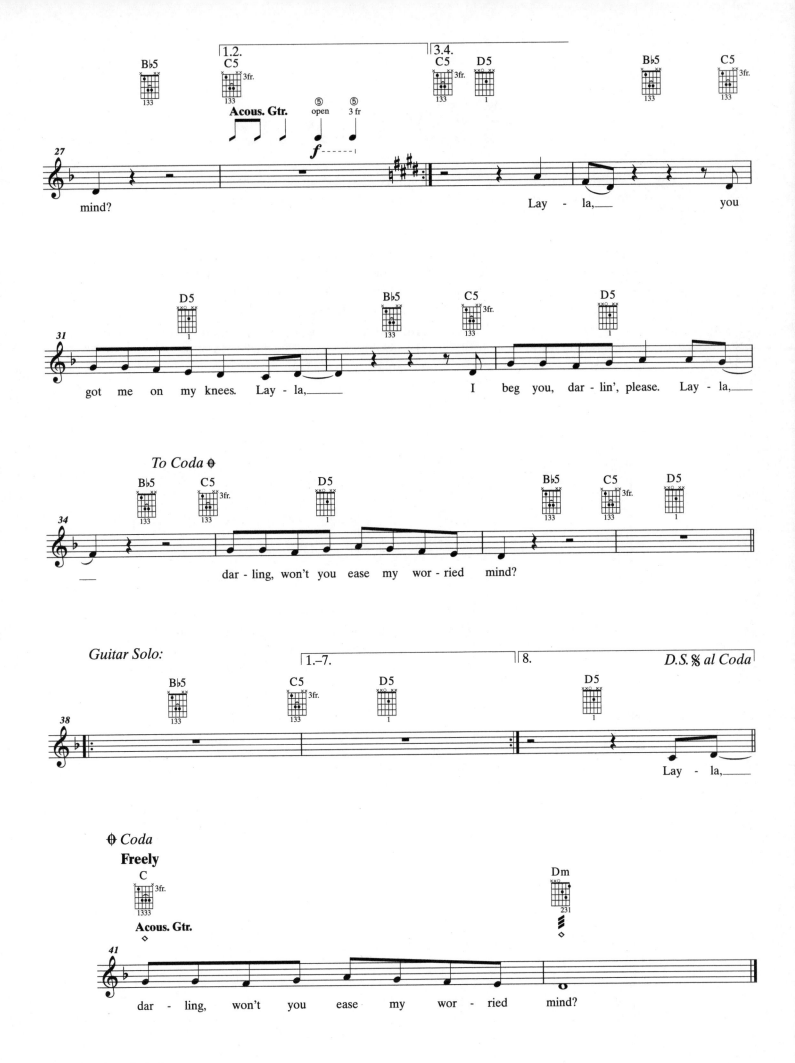

A Love Song

"A Love Song" was not a hit for Loggins & Messina, but Anne Murray's cover recording proved to be very successful, and a good follow-up to her rendition of Kenny Loggins's "Danny's Song."

This song has a fairly simple fingerstyle pattern with an alternating bass. In the notation, the bass notes all have stems facing down, and the standard *p i m a* abbreviations are placed next to the notes to indicate which right-hand fingers to use. (For an explanation of *p i m a*, see the lesson for "Can't Find My Way Home.")

Let's learn the pattern using a D chord, starting with just the alternating bass. All of the notes in the example below are played with the thumb. Count "1 2 3 4" in an even quarter-note rhythm as you repeat the sequence D–A–D–A.

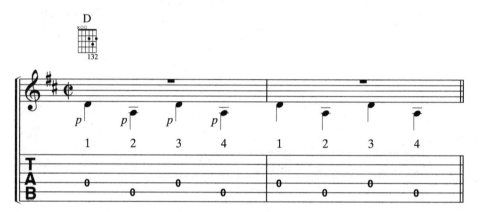

Once you're comfortable playing the bass part, we're ready to insert the notes played with the other right-hand fingers. While your thumb will be migrating from string to string on the alternating bass, the other fingers of your right hand are pretty much planted on their respective assigned strings: *i* always plays the 3rd string, *m* always plays the 2nd string, and *a* always plays the 1st string. Note that the first beat has a pinch of two notes played simultaneously: your middle finger plucks the 2nd-string D as your thumb plays the 4th-string D.

All the notes of this pattern fall into this rhythm: 1–2&–3&–4.

Tip

Try counting the rhythm out loud before you even pick up the guitar. Vocalizing rhythm is a good way to work out the beats before tackling the notes.

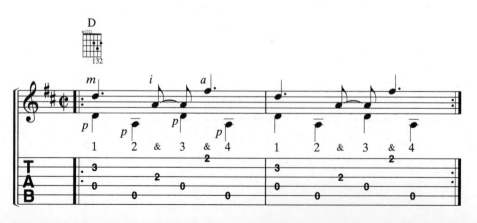

Don't jump the gun and start switching chords yet. Repeat the previous pattern on a D chord until you can do it in your sleep. Once the pattern is firmly ingrained into your muscle memory, slowly begin to introduce the other chords.

In measure 5, there is a double-stop hammer-on using the 2nd and 4th strings. Resist the tendency to use your left-hand 1st finger on the 4th string and your 2nd finger on the 2nd string for this hammer-on. Instead, use your 2nd finger on the 4th string and your 3rd finger on the 2nd string, because this will put your hand in position for the A chord that immediately follows. Like playing pool, playing guitar is often a matter of setting up your next shot.

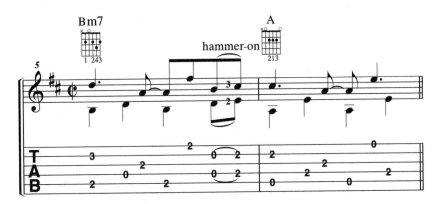

Guitar Gods

When singer-songwriter **KENNY LOGGINS** met producer **JIM MESSINA** in the early '70s, the two immediately hit it off. Loggins had moved from Washington to Los Angeles to become a staff songwriter, and found immediate success writing hits for the Nitty Gritty Dirt Band. His talents caught the ears and eyes of Messina who agreed to produce Loggins's debut album. Eventually, the two decided to go beyond the mere producer-performer relationship and became a duo: Loggins & Messina. The Loggins & Messina combo released hit after hit in the '70s, starting with *Kenny Loggins with Jim Messina Sittin' In* (1972) and *Loggins & Messina* (1972). *Full Sail* (1973) included the hit "A Love Song," which is a fine example of the cheerful, sensitive sound the duo had developed as their signature. Unfortunately, after the 1976 release of *Native Sons*, Loggins & Messina decided to go their separate ways and resumed solo careers.

A LOVE SONG

Words and Music by
KENNY LOGGINS and DONA LYN GEORGE

*Capo 2nd fret to match recording.

Moderately slow ♩ = 74

Intro:

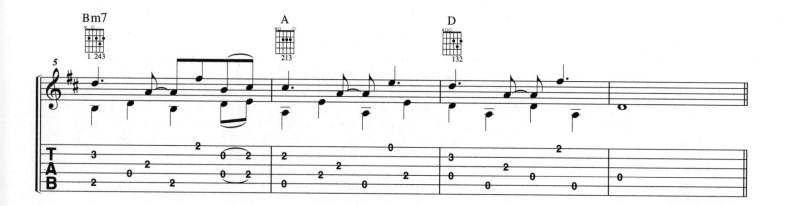

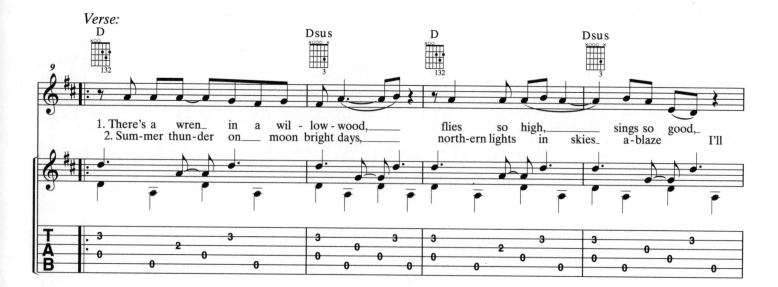

1. There's a wren_ in a wil - low - wood,_____ flies so high,_____ sings so good,_
2. Sum-mer thun-der on_ moon bright days,_____ north-ern lights in skies_ a-blaze I'll

A Love Song - 4 - 1

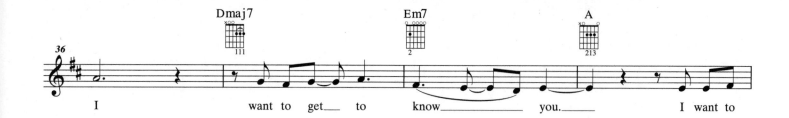

I want to get to know you. I want to

show you from the peace-ful feel-ing of my home.

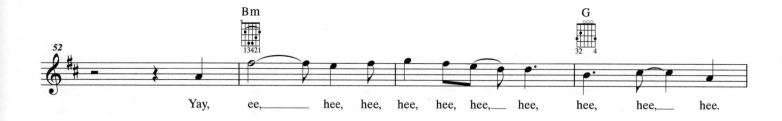

Bridge:

Yeah, ee, hee, hee, hee, hee, hee, hee, hee, hee, hee.

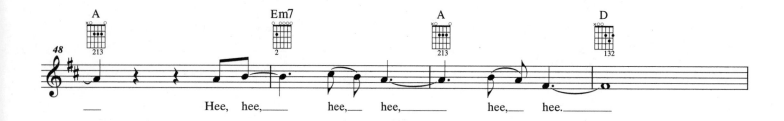

Hee, hee, hee, hee, hee, hee.

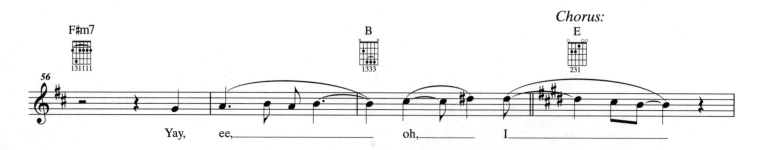

Yay, ee, hee, hee, hee, hee, hee, hee, hee, hee, hee.

Chorus:

Yay, ee, oh, I

A Love Song - 4 - 3

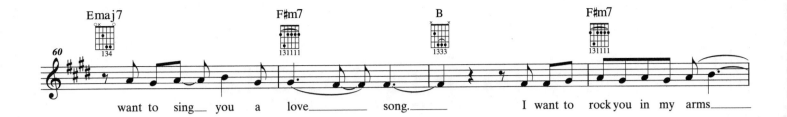

want to sing___ you a love_____ song._____ I want to rock you in my arms___

___ all_____ night long._____ I_____

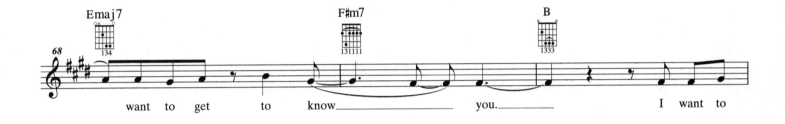

want to get to know_____ you._____ I want to

show you the peace - ful feel - ing of my home._____

Outro:

Oh, la, la, la, la._____ Oh, la, la, la, la,_____ la, la,___ la, la,

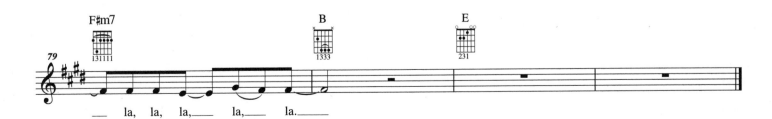

___ la, la, la,___ la,___ la._____

Margaritaville

Key Thoughts

Take Note

"Margaritaville" isn't a set of coordinates on a map, it's a state of mind. Jimmy Buffett and his legions of "Parrotheads" (the fans who've adopted his music and his message) live there, on the beach, basking in the sun.

This is a classic three-chord song. The only chords you need to know to play this song are D, G, and A. In the music, you will see a few variations on these three chords, like Dsus and A7. Add those only if you can play the basic D and A with total confidence.

This is a strumming song. Hold your pick loosely (but don't drop it!), and swing your wrist in a very steady up-and-down motion, which should be in perfect timing to the up-and-down tapping of your foot. Don't strike the strings on every strum or it will sound too busy. Instead, play on most of the down-strums and some of the up-strums. Find a rhythm that works for you and makes it easy for you to sing the song. The diagram below is just one suggestion for a simple strum pattern.

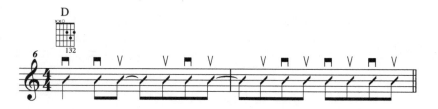

The four-measure introduction is the signature guitar part of this song. By the time you've played the first few beats, everyone will know you're in "Margaritaville." To play the pattern, lock your 1st finger down on the 1st string (the high E), and practice playing just the notes on the 1st string. Follow the TAB, and use your ear to guide you in playing the correct rhythm. Once you can play the melody on the 1st string with one finger, place your 3rd finger down on the 2nd string, lock your 1st and 3rd fingers into this position, and again use your 1st finger to guide this two-finger "grip" as shown in the TAB. All the notes that are two frets apart are played with a 1st- and 3rd-finger grip. In the third measure, use a 1st- and 2nd-finger grip to play the notes that are one fret apart (7–8 and 2–3). Your 1st finger should never leave the 1st string.

🎼 Tip

Once you find a good strum, don't keep changing it. Keep it steady and consistent!

🌸 Fun Fact

Legendary investment guru, billionaire, and mega-philanthropist Warren Buffett is Jimmy's first cousin.

MARGARITAVILLE

Margaritaville - 3 - 1

Verse 2:
Don't know the reason,
I stayed here all season
With nothing to show but this brand-new tattoo.
But it's a real beauty,
A Mexican cutie,
How it got here I haven't a clue.
(To Chorus:)

Verse 4:
I blew out my flip-flop,
Stepped on a pop-top;
Cut my heel, had to cruise on back home.
But there's booze in the blender,
And soon it will render
That frozen concoction that helps me hang on.
(To Chorus:)

***Verse 3:**
Old men in tank tops
Cruising the gift shops
Checking out the chiquitas down by the shore.
They dream about weight loss,
Wish they could be their own boss.
Those three-day vacations become such a bore.

**"Lost" verse (Live version only)*

Mr. Bojangles

Key Thoughts

"Mr. Bojangles" was originally written and performed by folk legend Jerry Jeff Walker. It became a folk-rock standard, though, so it's been covered by everyone from Chet Atkins to Sammy Davis Jr. The most popular version is by the Nitty Gritty Dirt Band, and this is the one we've used as the basis of our arrangement. Before trying to play it, be sure to listen to the original recording in order to make learning easier, and to ensure you get the right feel.

Take Note

The song is played with a *shuffle* rhythm in waltz time ¾. Shuffle, like *swing*, is based on an uneven eighth-note rhythm. The eighth-note pairs are played long-short, rather than both notes being of equal duration. If you're not sure what this means, get the recording and listen—that's by far the best way to get the feel.

The opening four bars are probably the most recognizable part of the song. Hold the simple G chord on the top three strings as shown in the TAB and the chord diagrams. Beneath that chord is a simple descending bass line on the 4th string: G–F#–E–D. Use your pick to play the 4th-string bass line, your middle finger *m* to play the note D on the 2nd string, and your ring finger *a* to play the note G on the 1st string.

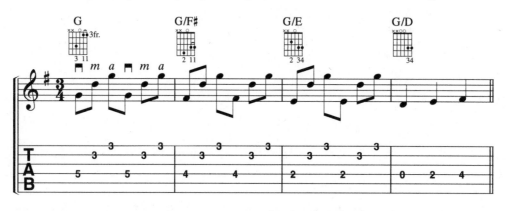

After the intro, the guitar part is basically a simple waltz strum pattern. Play the bass note of the chord on beat 1, then strum the rest of the chord on beats 2 and 3. Break up the strum with quarter notes and eighth notes as shown below.

Fun Fact

"Mr. Bojangles" is a classic story song based loosely on the life of Bill "Bojangles" Robinson, the legendary tap dancer from the early twentieth century.

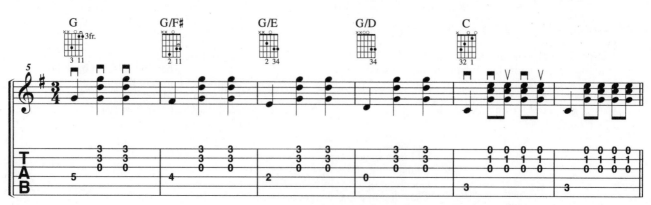

MR. BOJANGLES

Words and Music by
JERRY JEFF WALKER

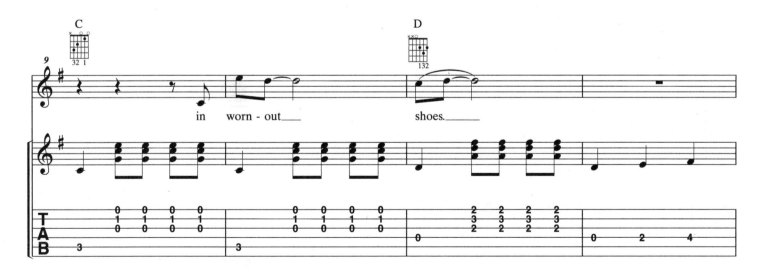

Mr. Bojangles - 3 - 1

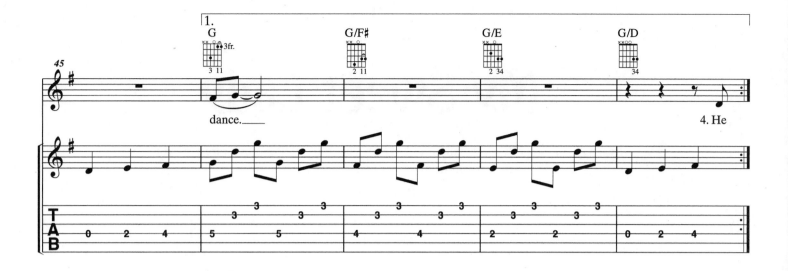

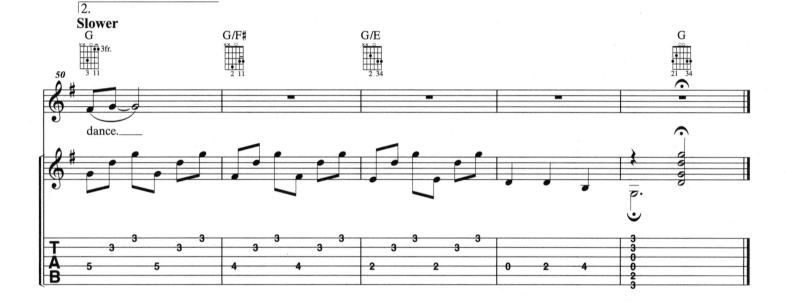

Verse 2:
I met him in a cell in New Orleans.
I was down and out.
He looked to me to be
The eyes of age
As he spoke right out.
He talked of life.
He talked of life.
He laughed, clicked his heels and stepped.
(To Chorus:)

Verse 3:
He said his name, "Bojangles," and he danced a lick
Across the cell.
He grabbed his pants and spread his stance,
Woah, he jumped so high
And then he clicked his heels.
He let go a laugh.
He let go a laugh,
Shook back his clothes all around.
(To Chorus:)

Verse 4:
He danced for those in minstrel shows and county fairs
Throughout the South.
He spoke through tears of fifteen years,
How his dog and him
Travelled about.
The dog up and died.
He up and died.
After twenty years, he still grieves.

Verse 5:
He said, "I've danced now
At every chance in honky-tonk
For drinks and tips.
But most the time was spent behind these county bars
'Cause I drinks a bit."
He shook his head.
And as he shook his head,
I heard someone ask him, "Please, please"…
(To Chorus:)

Mr. Bojangles - 3 - 3

My Sweet Lady

Key Thoughts

Learning to play this arrangement of "My Sweet Lady" will demonstrate how you can develop a really interesting guitar part just by moving a few notes from one chord to the next.

Take Note

This song is played very slowly and uses some simple chord shapes, so it's perfect for learning to fingerpick. The first example below shows the four-measure introduction. Notice that each chord is made of three notes on the top three strings, played over an open 4th-string D bass note.

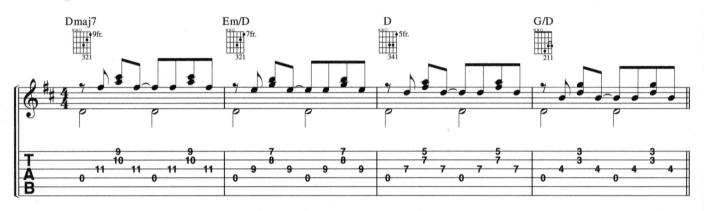

As previously mentioned, this song makes great use of simple chord movements. The next example shows you most of the chords to the verse. Just apply the fingerpicking pattern you learned in the introduction to each of these chord voicings, and you pretty much have the whole song!

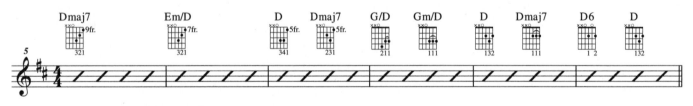

Guitar Gods

MY SWEET LADY

Words and Music by
JOHN DENVER

My Sweet Lady - 3 - 1

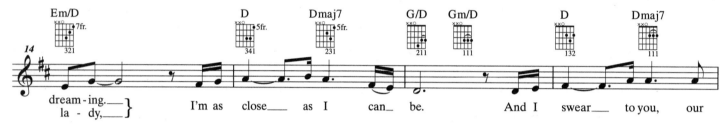

prom-ise   I will stay   right here   be - side   you.   To -

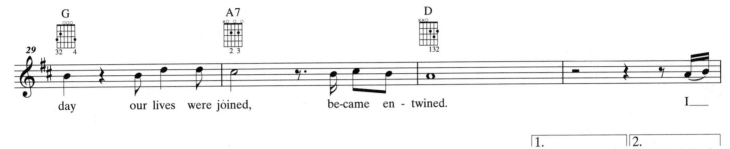

day   our lives were joined,   be-came en - twined.   I

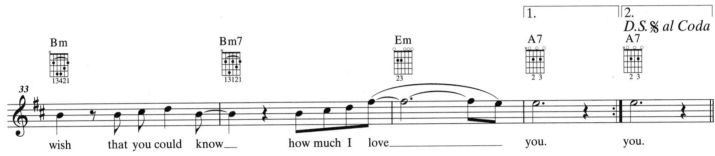

wish   that you could   know   how much I   love   you.   you.

time   has just   be - gun.

harm.

Verse 2:
Lady, are you happy?
Do you feel the way I do?
Are there meanings that you've never seen before?
Lady, my sweet lady,
I just can't believe it's true.
And it's like I've never ever loved before.
(To Bridge:)

Never Going Back Again

Key Thoughts

Lindsey Buckingham used this song to develop his Travis picking technique, which is named for country great Merle Travis. It is a fingerpicking technique in which the right hand thumb *never* stops playing quarter notes, constantly alternating between two strings. This technique can seem tricky at first, but once you get the hang of it, it's pretty easy. Your right hand begins to play the pattern automatically, and then you just have to change the left hand chords as needed.

Take Note

Before starting to play, you need to tune your low E string down a whole step to D. This is known as *Drop D tuning*, and is a very common variation on standard tuning. Next, if you want to match the key of the original recording, place a capo at the fourth fret.

Before attempting the Travis pattern, start by playing just the thumb pattern shown in the first example below. Keep playing it until your thumb goes on automatic. Try watching TV with a guitar in your lap and just play the pattern over and over.

Now we'll add the fingers. Always use your thumb to play the alternating bass-line notes, your index finger *i* on the 3rd string, your middle finger *m* on the 2nd string, and your ring finger *a* on the 1st string.

The first measure of this pattern uses a pinch technique. While your thumb continues to play on each quarter note, your middle finger plays a note at the same time on beats 2 and 4: you "pinch" the bass note and the top note between your thumb and finger. The second measure is more complicated. It requires playing notes in between thumb strokes. Practice the two-bar example below until your fingers can play it without your brain having to think about it.

One of the most recognizable parts of this song is the way Lindsey gets a constant "rolling" pattern going, as in the two bars below. The A13 (no 3rd) chord is a bit of a stretch. Hold the chord, get the alternating thumb pattern going, and then add the pinches and the in-between notes with your fingers.

Guitar Gods

FLEETWOOD MAC actually started out as an English blues trio formed by guitar player Peter Green in the 1960s, but Green departed, Christine McVie joined, and the Fleetwood Mac we all came to know was formed in 1975 when the soft-rock duo of Stevie Nicks and Lindsey Buckingham joined the group. The new members helped turn the band into hit makers just at the point when the band was about to become a thing of the past. The quintet's second album was the blockbuster *Rumours*. Released in 1977, *Rumours* reached No. 1 and stayed there for 31 weeks. The album eventually sold over 17 million copies, making it one of the best-selling albums of all time.

The story of the making of *Rumours* is legendary. The album was recorded while every member of the band was going through a personal crisis: Mick Fleetwood divorced his wife right before the recording sessions, and both of the couples in the band (John and Christine McVie, and Buckingham and Nicks) were breaking up. Songs like "Go Your Own Way," "Never Going Back Again," "Dreams," and "You Make Loving Fun" (this last written by Christine McVie about the man she was having an affair with) come off like journal entries. The term "confessional" music was probably never so appropriate, and the fact that the album was recorded at all is extraordinary. It is no wonder why *Rumours* continues to appeal to just about everyone, with its nearly universal themes served on a platter of easy-listening pop music.

NEVER GOING BACK AGAIN

Words and Music by
LINDSEY BUCKINGHAM

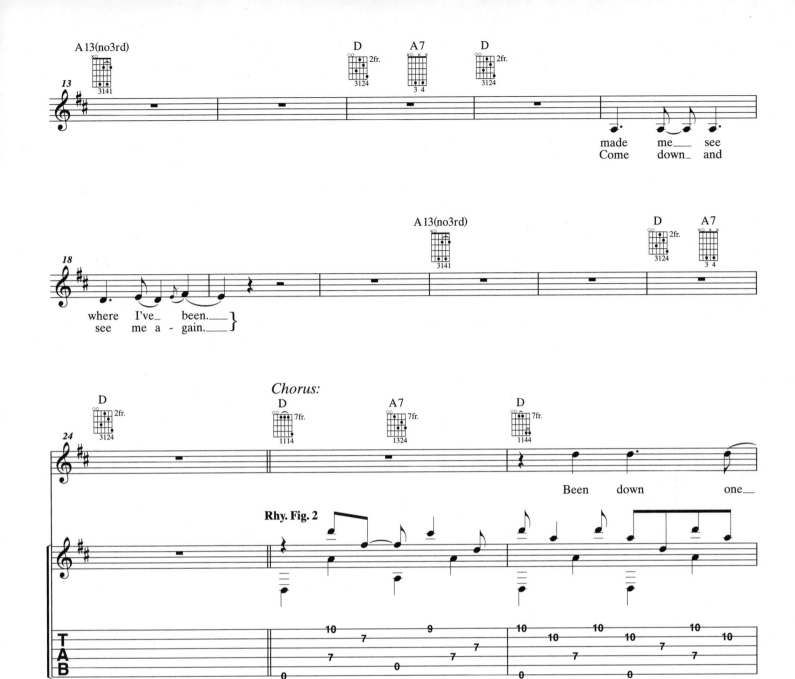

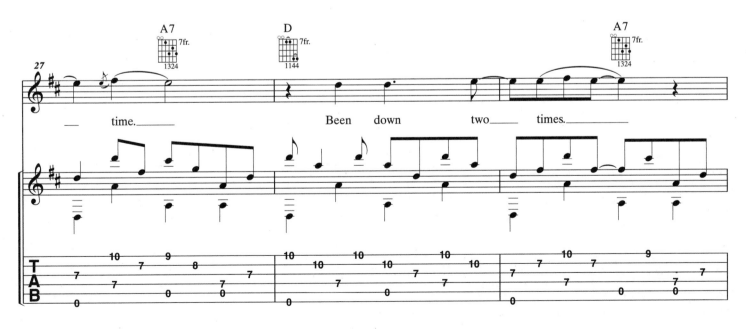

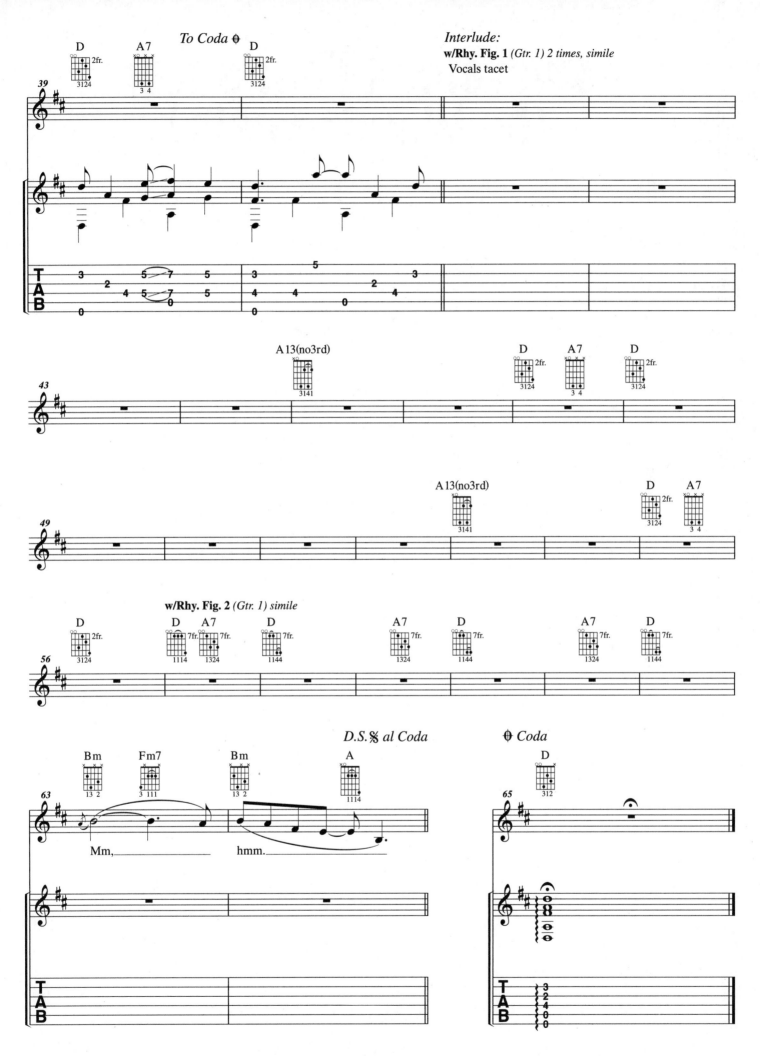

Operator (That's Not the Way It Feels)

Key Thoughts

"Operator" is one of Jim Croce's biggest hits. Like many of Jim's best works, it is a classic story song, this time about someone asking the phone operator's help in contacting a lost love. Maybe Jim was inspired a little by Chuck Berry's "Memphis," another great song with a similar storyline.

Take Note

As with all of Jim Croce's great ballads, the original recording has two beautifully interwoven guitar parts. Our arrangement presents a slightly simplified version of Jim's part, which is the lower of the two. If you listen to Jim Croce's recording with headphones, you'll hear Jim's guitar on the right and Maury Muehleisen's guitar playing higher harmony on the left.

The four-bar intro figure is played fingerstyle, and pretty much sums up the whole part. Use your thumb to play the down-stem bass notes and your fingers to play the up-stem notes. Make sure to plant your index, middle, and ring fingers on the top three strings.

For the verse and chorus, use a fingerpicking pattern similar to the intro. The third measure of the verse is simple quarter-note chords, and the fourth measure is a little countermelody, as shown below.

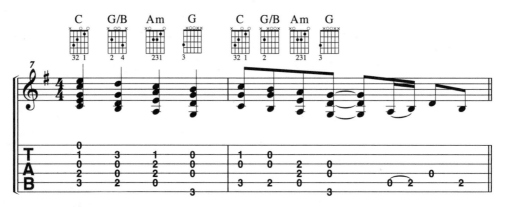

🌼 Fun Fact

1970 was the definitive decade of the singer/songwriter. Jim Croce ranks among the greatest in a long list that includes Jackson Browne, Carole King, Bob Dylan, Gordon Lightfoot, Joni Mitchell, Randy Newman, James Taylor, Neil Young, and Harry Nilsson. For a time, Croce gave up the music business to be a truck driver, and many of his story songs are influenced by his time spent on the road, at truck stops, and in trucker's bars.

OPERATOR (THAT'S NOT THE WAY IT FEELS)

Words and Music by
JIM CROCE

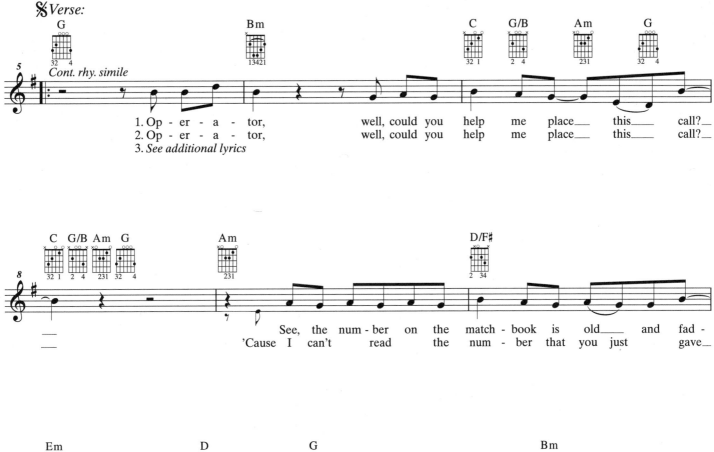

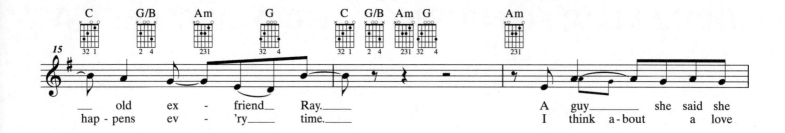

old ex - friend ___ Ray. ___ | A guy ___ she said she
hap - pens ev - 'ry ___ time. ___ | I think a - bout a love

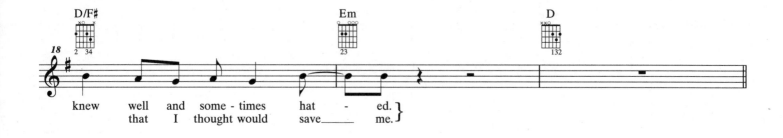

knew well and some - times hat - ed. ⎱
that I thought would save ___ me. ⎰

Chorus:

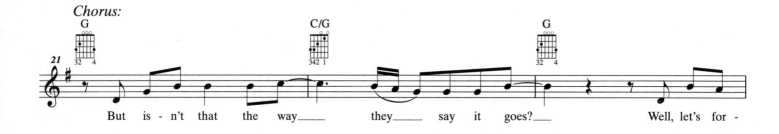

But is - n't that the way ___ they ___ say it goes? ___ Well, let's for -

get all that, ___ and give me the num - ber if you can find ___ it, so

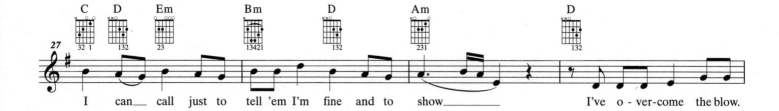

I can ___ call just to tell 'em I'm fine and to show ___ I've o - ver - come the blow.

I've learned to take it well, I on - ly wish my words ___ could just con - vince my - self

Operator (That's Not the Way It Feels) - 3 - 2

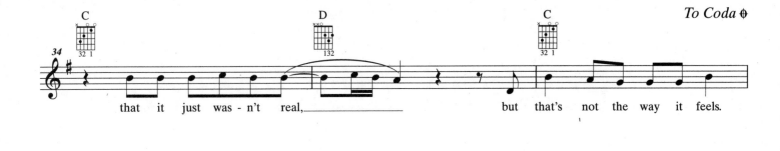

that it just was-n't real,_____ but that's not the way it feels.

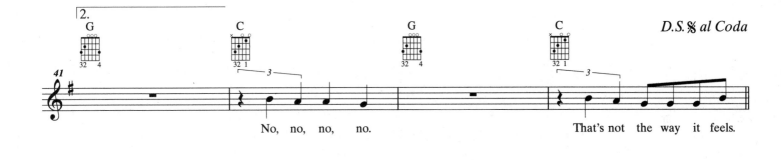

1.

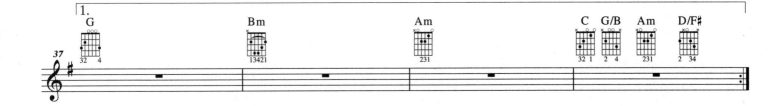

2.

D.S. 𝄋 al Coda

No, no, no, no.

That's not the way it feels.

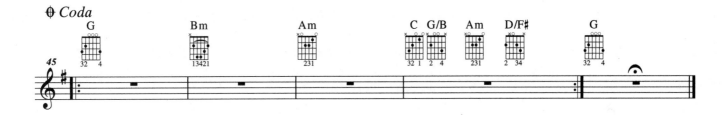

⊕ *Coda*

Verse 3:
Operator, well, let's forget about this call.
There's no one there I really wanted to talk to.
Thank you for your time, ah, you've been so much more than kind.
You can keep the dime.
(To Chorus:)

Peaceful Easy Feeling

Key Thoughts

The list of amazing hits from Eagles seems endless at times, but perhaps more than any other song, "Peaceful Easy Feeling" helped define their quintessential, southern California sound. The song almost demands to be listened to in the car—top down, cruising the Pacific Coast Highway in Malibu.

Take Note

This is another classic strumming song—just a few basic chords, a simple strum pattern, and a little Malibu sunshine. For a good strum technique, hold the pick loosely between your thumb and index finger and swing your wrist in a constant down-up pattern. Strum all the strings of each chord on the down-stroke, but the up-stroke should only catch the top three strings. This happens pretty naturally if you are strumming from your wrist with a loose, arc-like motion.

The introduction is simply E to Esus as shown below. Use similar strumming patterns throughout the whole song.

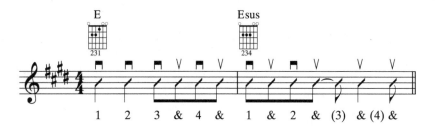

Whenever you move from one chord to the next, try to find a common note or some other way a finger can be used as a pivot point. This makes for smooth and easy chord changes, such as the move from E to A in the verse. In this case, you can use the 1st finger as a pivot point. From the E chord, slide your 1st finger up from the first fret to the second fret and, as you slide, release your 2nd and 3rd fingers from the 4th and 5th strings and reposition them on the 4th and 2nd strings to form the A chord. Changing from A to E is simply the same process in reverse. This chord change is illustrated in the following example. Notice the accents on beats 2 and 4 of the constant eighth-note strum pattern as well. Play the accents as shown, and experiment with different patterns by sounding and muting chords on various beats.

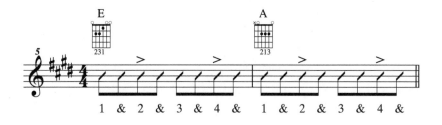

Guitar Gods

Released in June 1972, **EAGLES's** self-titled debut introduced the world to Glenn Frey, Don Henley, Bernie Leadon, and Randy Meisner. *Eagles* made the Top 20 and eventually reached gold with the hits "Take It Easy," "Witchy Woman," and "Peaceful Easy Feeling." This rock and roll/country/folk-influenced LP is known for its nearly equal songwriting efforts from all members of the group, and even includes songs co-written by greats such as Jackson Browne ("Take It Easy"), Gene Clark ("Train Leaves Here This Morning"), and Jack Tempchin ("Peaceful Easy Feeling"). Several songs from this record are prominently featured on the best-selling album of all time, *Eagles: Their Greatest Hits 1971–1975*.

PEACEFUL EASY FEELING

Words and Music by
JACK TEMPCHIN

Moderate country rock

1. I like the way your spark - lin' ear - rings lay

2.3. *See additional lyrics*

a - gainst your skin so brown.

And I wan - na sleep with you in the des - ert to - night,

with a bil - lion stars all a - round. 'Cause I got a

Chorus:

peace - ful eas - y feel - in',

and I know you won't let me down, 'cause I'm

Peaceful Easy Feeling - 2 - 1

Verse 2:
And I found out a long time ago
What a woman can do to your soul.
Ah, but she can't take you anyway,
You don't already know.
(To Chorus:)

Verse 3:
I get this feelin' I may know you
As a lover and a friend.
But this voice keeps whispering in my other ear,
Tells me I may never see you again.
(To Chorus:)

Photographs & Memories

Key Thoughts

"Photographs & Memories" may not be Jim Croce's most well-known song, but it is one of his most beautiful. Like most really beautiful songs, it's very simple—just a pretty melody, a basic set of chords, and a touching lyric.

Take Note

Most of this song is based on a simple, repetitive two-chord progression of Gmaj7 and Cmaj7. The major 7th chords set off the melancholy tone of the lyrics perfectly.

Once you've learned the two-measure introduction, you've learned most of the song, since these measures repeat throughout the verses. If you don't read music, don't worry—this is easy. Just hold the Gmaj7 chord as shown in the diagram, and then pick out the strings one at a time as shown in the TAB. Do the same for the Cmaj7 chord in the second measure. If you don't know how this is supposed to sound, get a recording of the song right away. Once you listen to the guitar part, it will come together very fast.

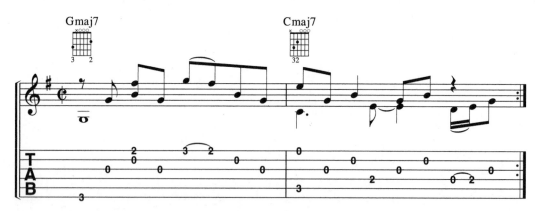

Most of the guitar part for each verse is the same as the intro. Easy! After the intro figure is played twice, each verse ends with Am, Bm, Em, and D7. Just keep fingerpicking each chord in a simple, steady eighth-note pattern.

One of the greatest parts to this song is the surprise chord in the last measure of the chorus. It's just a simple F#m barre chord, but it comes out of nowhere—which is the genius of it—and adds the perfect unresolved, melancholy feeling required to complement the lyric.

Guitar Gods

JIM CROCE was one of the great songwriters of his era, and the amazingly interwoven dual-guitar parts he recorded with his lead guitarist, Maury Muehleisen, set a whole new standard for acoustic guitar recordings. Many of his songs were story songs. Some, like "Photographs & Memories" and "Operator," tell stories of lost love, while others such as "Bad, Bad Leroy Brown" and "You Don't Mess Around with Jim" are humorous tales of larger-than-life characters.

After kicking around a number of odd jobs that ranged from performing in local bands throughout the Philadelphia area to writing jingles for a radio station, construction, working with deprived children, and a stint in the Army, Croce moved to New York in the mid-1960s to get serious about performing his music. He and his wife, Ingrid, performed together on the coffeehouse circuit for a few years, until, discouraged with New York, they returned to Pennsylvania and survived off Ingrid's baking and crafts while Jim sold off his collection of instruments.

In the early '70s, Croce finally released his first album, *You Don't Mess Around with Jim*, which spawned three major hits: the title track, "Operator," and "Bad, Bad Leroy Brown." Eventually, more than two million copies were sold. His next album, *I Got a Name*, featured the huge hit single "Time in a Bottle," but he would never see his song top the charts. On September 20, 1973, following a concert at Northwestern State University in Louisiana, his small charter plane crashed while taking off in bad weather. Both he and Muehleisen were killed in the crash.

PHOTOGRAPHS & MEMORIES

Words and Music by
JIM CROCE

Pho-to - graphs and mem-o - ries,___ Christ-mas cards you sent to me.___

All that I have are these___ to re - mem-ber you.

2. Mem-o - ries___ that come at night, take me to an - oth - er time.___
4. Pho-to - graphs_ and mem - o - ries, all the love you gave to me.___

Back to a hap - pi - er day___ when I called you mine.___
Some - how it just can't be true,___ that's all I've left of you.___ But

Photographs & Memories - 2 - 1

Ripple

Key Thoughts

"Ripple" is one of the best-known and easiest-to-play songs from the legendary Grateful Dead. Jerry Garcia's introductory guitar part is very similar to *Carter style*, a guitar style made famous by Mother Maybelle Carter, matriarch of the royal family of country music that also includes June Carter, Johnny Cash, and Rosanne Cash.

Take Note

"Ripple" is played with a shuffle feel (see the lesson for "Mr. Bojangles"). If you're not sure how to create the shuffle feel, get the recording and listen—it's by far the best way to learn this or any other rhythmic feel.

The accompaniment pattern is a very simple acoustic strumming part that really shows Jerry Garcia's early bluegrass roots. To play the accompaniment during the verses and chorus, just play a basic alternating bass-strum pattern as shown below. (This kind of alternating bass pattern is often called a "boom-chick" pattern.) Since there are only four chords in the song, we've given you the alternating pattern for each one. Repeat each measure until you can play it smoothly without interruption.

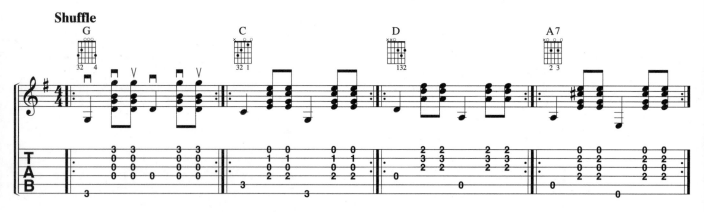

Guitar Gods

One of the most beloved and followed jam bands of the '60s and '70s, **GRATEFUL DEAD** spread peace and love through music everywhere they went. In 1967, they released their self-titled debut on Warner Bros. Records, but with not nearly the acclaim they had expected given the legions of "Deadheads" that followed the band. Some experimentation on how to present Grateful Dead on a record resulted in three more releases in the late 1960s. Then, 1970 saw the release of *Working Man's Dead* and *American Beauty*. These two albums contained some of the Dead's biggest hits such as "Casey Jones," "Truckin'," "Sugar Magnolia," and "Uncle John's Band," and their popularity established bluegrass as a part of mainstream rock music.

Once you can play all the chords with the preceding alternating bass pattern, you are ready to try the Carter-style intro. In Carter style, Maybelle Carter would play a melody in the bass of her guitar and then fill in the spaces between the melody notes with an alternating bass style. The effect is that it implies the sound of two guitars.

Following are the first five bars of the guitar intro. When playing in this style, always hold the indicated chord, pick out the melody notes, and use any other available finger to play notes not in the chord fingering. It is critical that you try to hold each full chord up until the next chord change. Below, we've indicated where to hold the chord and where to release in order to play a melodic passage.

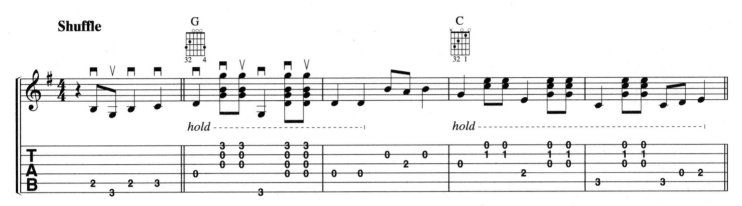

RIPPLE

Words by ROBERT HUNTER
Music by JERRY GARCIA

Moderate country shuffle
Intro:

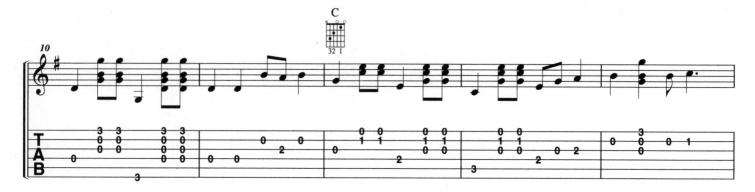

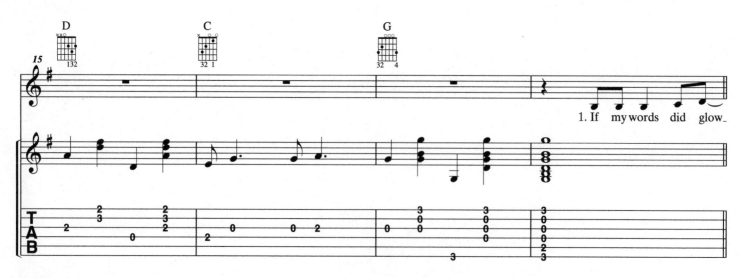

1. If my words did glow_

Ripple - 3 - 1

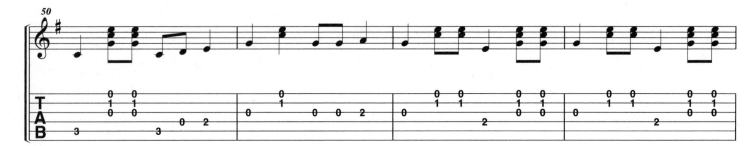

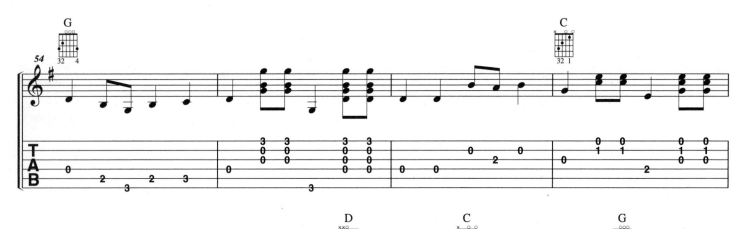

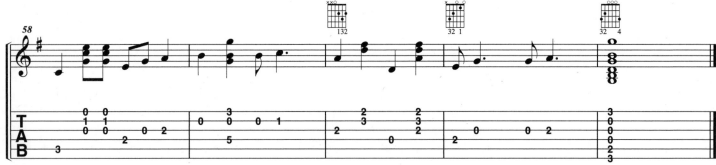

Verse 3:
Reach out your hand
If your cup is empty.
If your cup is full,
May it be again.
Let it be known,
There is a fountain
That was not made
By the hands of man.

Verse 4:
There is a road,
No simple highway,
Between the dawn
And the dark of night.
And if you go,
No one may follow.
That path is for
Your steps alone.
(To Chorus:)

Verse 5:
You who choose
To lead must follow.
But if you fall, you fall alone.
If you should stand,
Then who's to guide you?
If I knew the way,
I would take you home.

Scarborough Fair/ Canticle

Key Thoughts

In 1966, Paul Simon and Art Garfunkel fused two traditional folk songs together and added a uniquely beautiful fingerstyle guitar part. The result is one of the most iconic songs of the '60s.

Take Note

This song is in $\frac{3}{4}$. A typical $\frac{3}{4}$ fingerpicking pattern has six eighth notes with three strong beats per measure: **1** & **2** & **3** &. The "Scarborough Fair" pattern is in eighth notes, but because the finger pattern is played *p–a–i–p–m–i*, there is a natural tendency for some measures to feel as if there are only two strong beats as if in $\frac{6}{8}$: **1** 2 3 **4** 5 6. The melody clearly feels like $\frac{3}{4}$, but depending on the accents and the chord forms, some of the instrumental guitar breaks sound like they switch to $\frac{6}{8}$, which is one of the elements that gives the song its unique sound.

The intro sets up the opening pattern with a little descending bass line of D–C–B in the second and third measures. The two-measure pattern starting at bar 4 pretty much lays out the fingerpicking pattern for the whole song. Be careful to use the indicated fingerings, as shown below.

Capo 7th fret

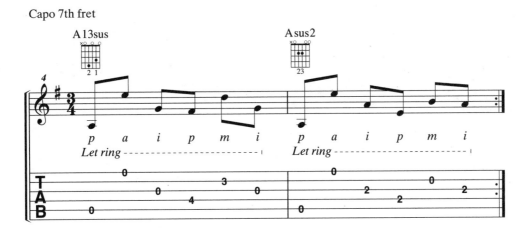

One more important point to make: For some songs, a capo is optional because it's only needed to match the recorded key. But because this song is so high up the neck (at the seventh fret), the capo is essential for getting the right sound. If you don't already have a capo, now is a good time to get one.

Guitar Gods

It took **PAUL SIMON** and **ART GARFUNKEL** three attempts before they hit their stride. After breaking up twice, Simon and Garfunkel finally found success with the 1966 album *Parsley, Sage, Rosemary and Thyme*, which included the classic "Scarborough Fair/Canticle." The duo broke up for good after the release of *Bridge Over Troubled Water* in 1970, but have reunited several times through the years for live performances. One of their most famous reunions was their 1981 concert in Central Park, which attracted over 500,000 fans.

SCARBOROUGH FAIR/CANTICLE

Capo 7th fret to match recording.

Arrangement and Original Countermelody by
PAUL SIMON and ARTHUR GARFUNKEL

Moderately ♩ = 126

Intro:

Verse:

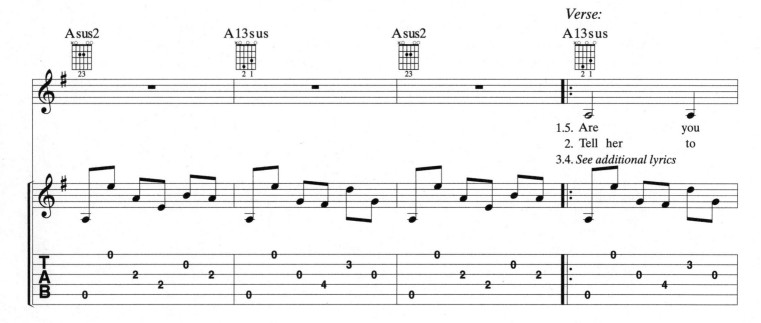

1.5. Are you
2. Tell her to
3.4. *See additional lyrics*

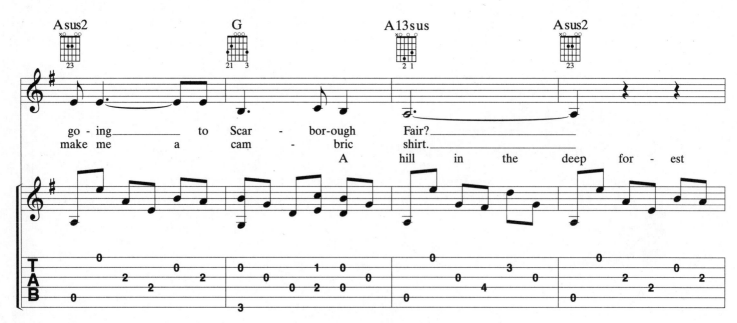

go - ing_____ to Scar - bor-ough Fair?_____
make me a cam - bric shirt._____
A hill in the deep for - est

Scarborough Fair/Canticle - 3 - 1

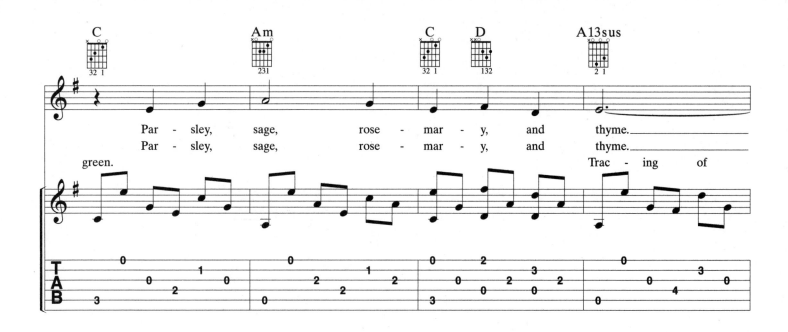

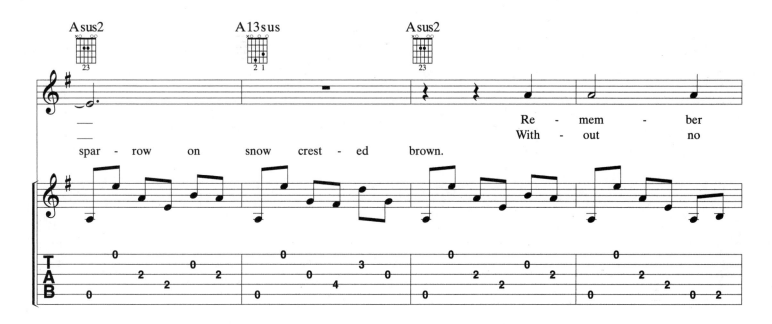

Scarborough Fair/Canticle - 3 - 2

Verse 3:
Tell her to find me an acre of land.
On the side of a hill a sprinkling of leaves.
Parsely, sage, rosemary, and thyme.
Washes the grave with silvery tears.
Between the salt water and the sea strand.
A soldier cleans and polishes a gun.
Then she'll be a true love of mine.
Sleeps unaware of the clarion call.

Verse 4:
Tell her to reap it in a sickle of leather.
War bellows blazing in scarlet battalions.
Parsley, sage, rosemary, and thyme.
Generals order their soldiers to kill.
And gather it all in a bunch of heather.
And to fight for a cause they've long ago forgotten.
Then she'll be a true love of mine.

Sister Golden Hair

Key Thoughts

"Sister Golden Hair" is a perfect song for getting your strumming patterns together. Hold your pick loosely and swing your hand from the wrist. For the most part, keep a constant down-up strum motion going at all times. Follow the notated patterns, or use your ear to determine when to strike the strings and when to miss.

Take Note

In addition to being a great strumming song, "Sister Golden Hair" is perfect for learning many basic barre chord fingerings. Most of the chord changes are anticipated, meaning they are played on the "&" of beat 4, just before the downbeat of the next measure. For example, in the excerpt below, the A chord in the second measure is actually played on the "&" of beat 4 in bar 1, the E chord in measure 3 is played on the "&" of 4 in bar 2, and so on. If you are strumming with the correct down-up pattern, each anticipated chord change will occur on an up-stroke.

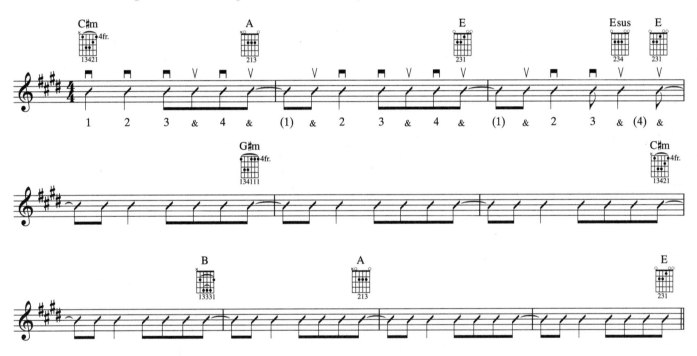

Fun Fact

The three original members of America met in England where their American fathers served in the U.S. military. Between 1974 and 1979, the band was produced by George Martin—legendary producer of the Beatles, so it's not too surprising that the slide guitar intro on "Sister Golden Hair" was directly inspired by George Harrison's "My Sweet Lord."

SISTER GOLDEN HAIR

Moderately fast ♩ = 134

Words and Music by
GERRY BECKLEY

3. Well, I keep

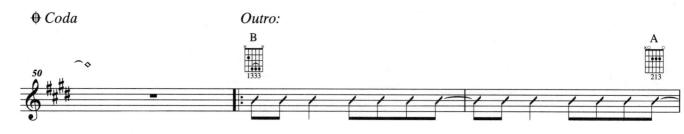

Sunshine on My Shoulders

Key Thoughts

The slow, gentle fingerstyle guitar part that John Denver used to accompany himself on this song is really ideal for learning to fingerpick. If you're new to fingerstyle—this is a good place to start. Even if you're not new to fingerstyle, the song is a fine lesson in simplicity, grace, and beauty.

Take Note

If you're listening to the recording as you learn this song (as we recommend you do for all the songs in this book), you may notice that the guitar has a very high "chimey" sound, almost like a harpsichord or a mandolin. That kind of sound is always a good indication that a capo is being used on the guitar. In this case, John has a capo at the third fret, so if you want to play along with the recording or sing in the same key, place a capo on the third fret of your guitar.

The introduction and chorus are based on the simplest of chord progressions: G to C. Play the introduction as shown below. Make sure to keep your left hand 4th finger locked on the 1st-string G for both chords.

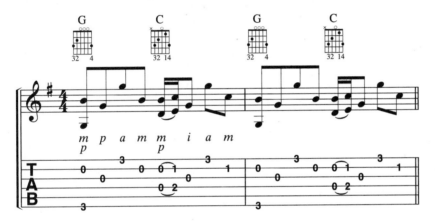

Bars 9 and 10 of the chorus move to Am and D7 chords. Below is a suggestion for one way to play through these chords. Hold each chord through the full measure and let it ring.

Okay, if you're ready for a bit of a challenge, the following example shows how to play the previous two measures by combining the chords with a moving bass line to fill space and create an interesting countermelody. Hold the 2nd-string C with your 1st finger throughout, and pick out the bass line with your right thumb as indicated.

The verse is built from four chords in the key of G, played in ascending sequence: G–Am–Bm–C. Here is a suggested pattern for playing through these chords.

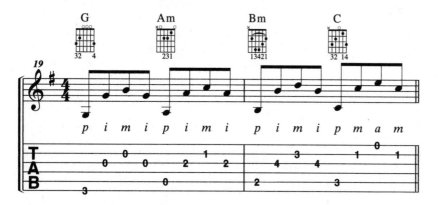

Guitar Gods

Clean-cut country singer/songwriter **JOHN DENVER** was actually born John Deutschendorf, but after getting his start in the local club scene while attending Texas Tech, he changed his name in homage to the area of Colorado he loved so much. In 1964, Denver relocated to L.A. to join the Chad Mitchell Trio. As the original members left the group, the name was changed to Denver, Boise, and Johnson. Just a short time later, Denver left to pursue his solo career. Two less-than-successful albums later, he released *Poems, Prayers & Promises* in 1971, with unbelievable results. Hits like the title track, "Take Me Home Country Roads," and "Sunshine on My Shoulders" sent the record shooting to No. 6 on the country charts and No. 15 on the pop charts, and "Take Me Home Country Roads" nearly topped the charts at No. 2.

SUNSHINE ON MY SHOULDERS

Words by
JOHN DENVER
Music by
JOHN DENVER, MIKE TAYLOR and DICK KNISS

Capo 3rd fret to match recording.

Moderately slow ♩ = 74

Sunshine on My Shoulders - 3 - 1

Sun-shine al-most al - ways_____ makes me high._____

Verse:

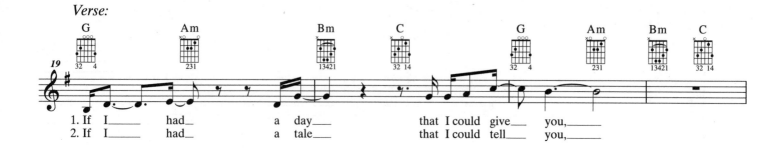

1. If I_____ had_____ a day_____ that I could give_____ you,_____
2. If I_____ had_____ a tale_____ that I could tell_____ you,_____

I'd give to you a day just like to - day._____
I'd tell a tale sure to make you smile._____

If I_____ had_____ a song_____ that I could sing_____ for you,_____
If I_____ had_____ a wish_____ that I could wish_____ for you,_____

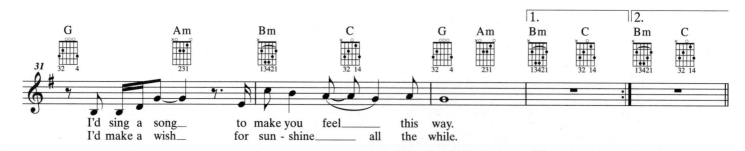

I'd sing a song_____ to make you feel_____ this way.
I'd make a wish_____ for sun - shine_____ all the while.

Take It Easy

Key Thoughts Co-written by Jackson Browne and Glenn Frey of Eagles, "Take It Easy" is a feel-good classic. The lyrics entwine two classic themes of rock and roll: girls and cars.

Take Note "Take it Easy" is a simple strumming song that uses all standard chords in the key of G: G, C, D, Em, and Am. Rhythm slashes throughout the intro show the acoustic guitar strum pattern for the whole song. An "x" notehead in the pattern (such as on beat 3 in the first measure) indicates a percussive sound rather than a chord strum. To create this effect, just keep strumming up and down with your pick, but lightly release the left-hand pressure on the strings for this beat.

This song has a signature electric lead guitar part, which is written out in the notation and TAB. You'll need an electric guitar with light gauge strings to play the double-stop bends in bar 9. If you play this part on an acoustic guitar, you probably won't be able to play the double-stop bends, so try this instead: place your 1st finger on the 3rd-string A and your 2nd finger on the 2nd-string D; strike both strings, and immediately hammer your 3rd finger down on the 3rd-string B. Here is the lick with this hammer-on technique.

Guitar Gods

Glenn Frey, Don Henley, Bernie Leadon, and Randy Meisner were signed as **EAGLES** by famed record producer David Geffen in September 1971, following a brief tour as Linda Ronstadt's band. The following year, the group took two weeks in England to record their self-titled debut, *Eagles*, which reached the Top 20 and eventually went gold with hits like "Take It Easy," "Witchy Woman," and "Peaceful Easy Feeling." From that very first record, Eagles spent their career releasing hit after hit and today hold the prestigious honor of having the best-selling record of all time, *Eagles: Their Greatest Hits 1971–1975*, which has sold over 29 million copies to date.

TAKE IT EASY

Words and Music by
JACKSON BROWNE
and GLENN FREY

Moderately ♩ = 138

Intro:

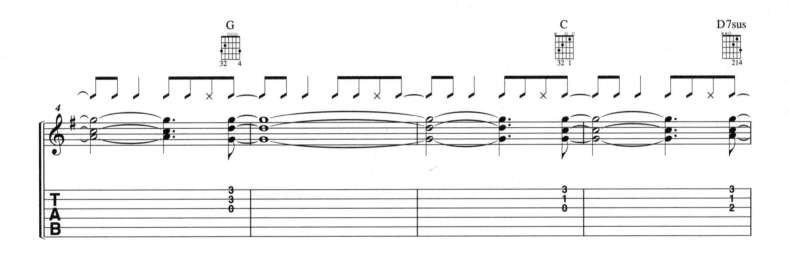

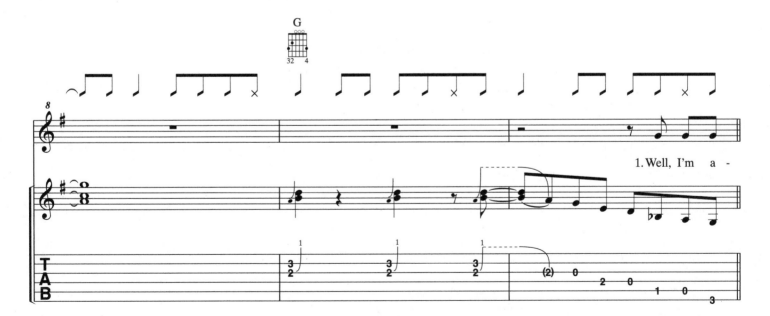

1. Well, I'm a -

Take It Easy - 5 - 1

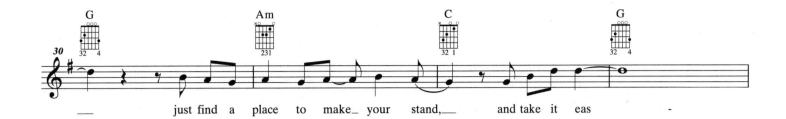

just find a place to make_ your stand,__ and take it eas

y.__ 2. Well, I'm a - y.__

Guitar Solo:

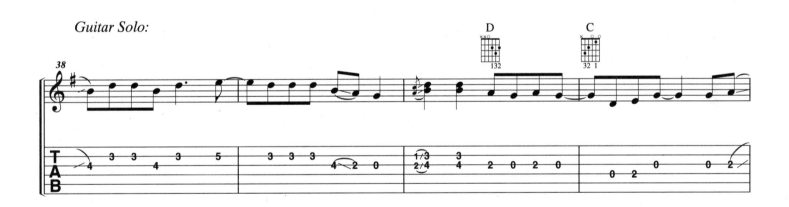

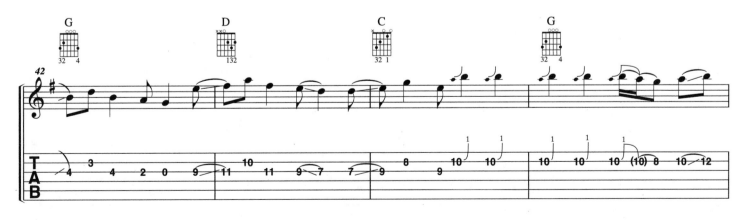

Take It Easy - 5 - 3

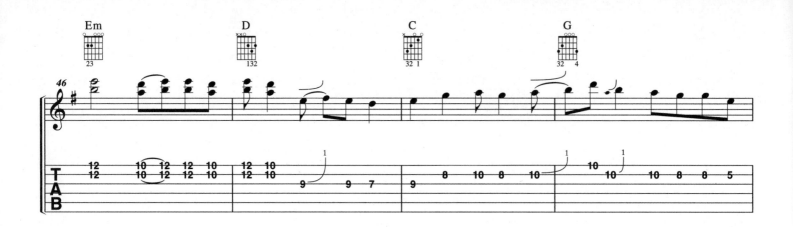

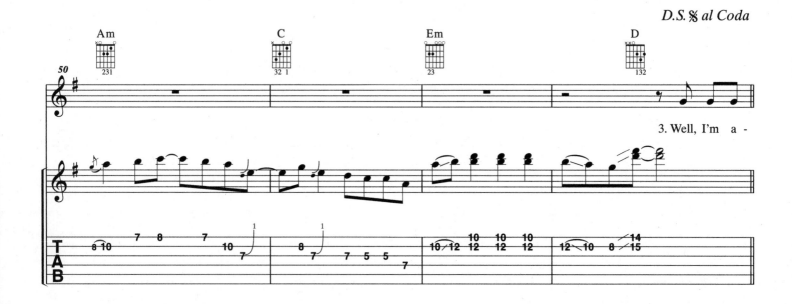

D.S. % al Coda

3. Well, I'm a -

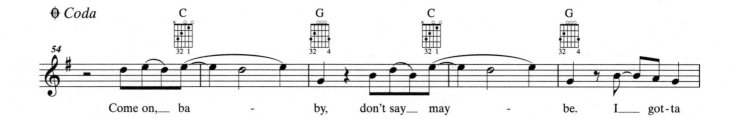

Come on,__ ba - by, don't say__ may - be. I__ got-ta

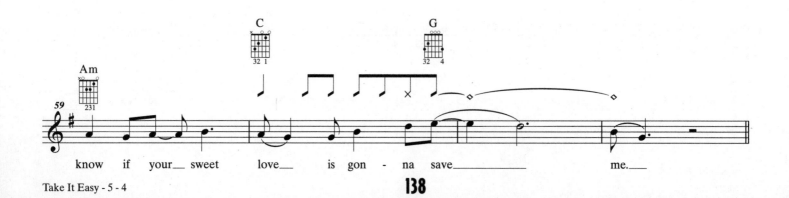

know if your__ sweet love__ is gon - na save_____ me.__

Outro:

Ooh,_____ ooh,_____ ooh,_____ ooh.____ Ooh,_____

ooh,_____ ooh,_____ ooh.____ Ooh,_____ Oh,__ we got it
(Ooh.____)

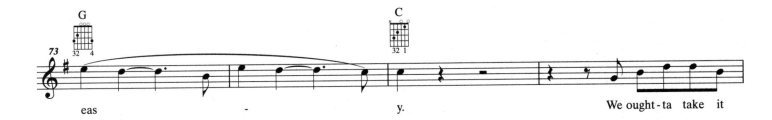

eas - y. We ought-ta take it

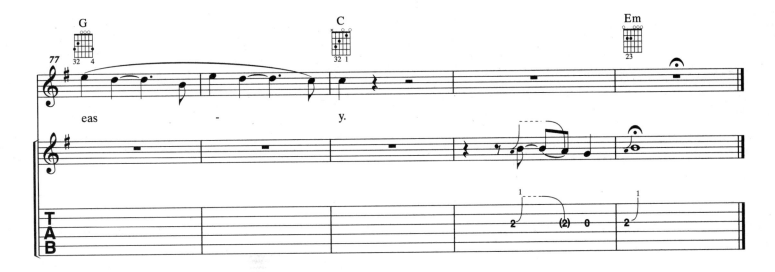

eas - y.

Verse 2:
Well, I'm a-standin' on a corner in Winslow, Arizona,
And such a fine sight to see:
It's a girl, my Lord, in a flatbed Ford
Slowin' down to take a look at me.

Chorus 2:
Come on, baby, don't say maybe.
I gotta know if your sweet love is gonna save me.
We may lose and we may win, though we will never be here again.
So open up, I'm climbin' in, so take it easy.
(To Guitar Solo:)

Verse 3:
Well, I'm a-runnin' down the road, tryin' to loosen my load,
Got a world of trouble on my mind.
Lookin' for a lover who won't blow my cover,
She's so hard to find.
(To Chorus:)

Taxi

 Key Thoughts

"Taxi" is one of the great story songs from the remarkable singer-songwriter and story-teller Harry Chapin. The signature guitar part is found in the first two measures. Once you've got them down, you're pretty much home free.

Take Note

The core of this song is formed by a two-measure fingerpicking pattern of alternating D and Am chords. Use the open E (the first note of the Am chord) as your opportunity to change chord fingerings without interrupting the flow. The fingerpicking pattern is shown below.

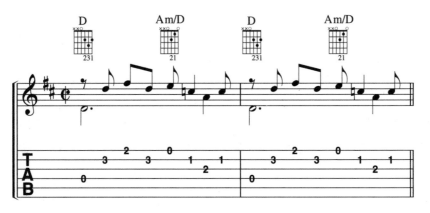

The strum marks above the melody starting at the 11th bar of the verse indicate where to switch from finger-picking to the indicated strum pattern. You can strum the chords with a pick or just use your thumb. At the chorus, we break into a fairly typical folk-style accompaniment using standard open-position chords.

Fun Fact

In 1986, Harry Chapin was post-humously awarded the Congressional Gold Medal in recognition of his humani-tarian efforts to alleviate hunger in the world.

TAXI

Moderately ♩ = 60

Intro:

Words and Music by
HARRY CHAPIN

Taxi - 7 - 1

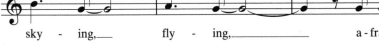

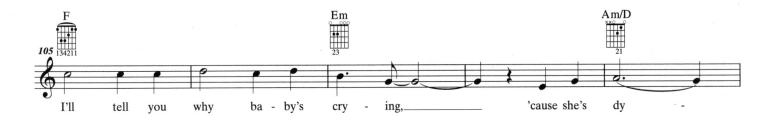

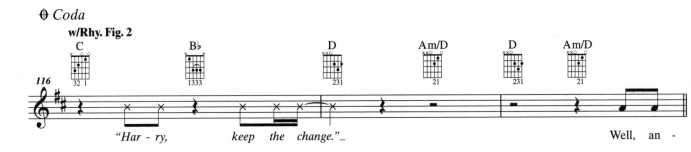

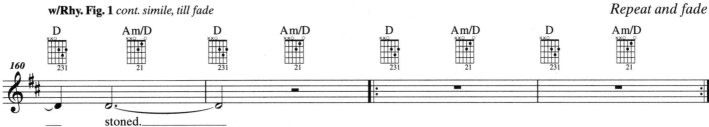

Verse 3:
Something about her was familiar;
I could swear I'd seen her face before.
But she said, "I'm sure you're mistaken."
And she didn't say anything more.

Verse 4:
It took a while, but she looked in the mirror,
Then she glanced at the license for my name.
A smile seemed to come to her slowly;
It was a sad smile just the same.
(To Verse 5:)

Verse 6:
There was not much more for us to talk about;
Whatever we had once was gone.
So I turned my cab into the driveway,
Past the gate and the fine-trimmed lawns.

Verse 7:
And she said, "We must get together,"
But I knew it'd never be arranged.
Then she handed me twenty dollars for a two-fifty fare;
She said, *(spoken)* "Harry, keep the change."
(To Verse 8:)

Wake Me Up When September Ends

"Wake Me Up When September Ends" is Billie Joe Armstrong's poignant remembrance of his father's passing when Billie was just 10 years old. It expresses his desire for respite from the pain that still persists after more than 20 years.

This elegiac tune opens with a simple picked pattern with *unison* G notes (the same pitch produced on different strings). The guitar part on the verse expands to a similar figure with a descending bass. The modulation from the C major chord to the C minor chord under the lyrics "when September ends" underscores the sad significance of the fall month.

On the repeats of measures 9–12 and 17–28, you may play an optional eighth-note rhythm with all down-strokes as notated below. Continue with all down-strokes on the eighth notes in the guitar solo.

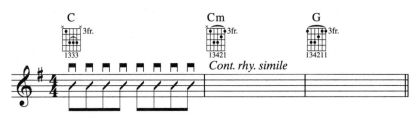

Guitar Gods

Rising from the northern California underground punk scene, **GREEN DAY** found mainstream success in the 1990s with albums rooted in a Ramones- and Buzzcocks-influenced brand of punk. After such a firm grounding in catchy, three-chord, punk-pop songs, the 2004 release *American Idiot* surprised everyone. A lyrically aggressive and politically charged rock opera, the album featured songs that were influenced by the political passion of bands like the Clash. It touched on timely issues of the day, featuring the singles "American Idiot," "Boulevard of Broken Dreams," "Holiday," and "Wake Me Up When September Ends." Possibly Green Day's career-defining album, *American Idiot* was the band's biggest critical success and established them as much more than just a punk band.

WAKE ME UP WHEN SEPTEMBER ENDS

Words by BILLIE JOE
Music by GREEN DAY

Wake Me Up When September Ends - 3 - 1

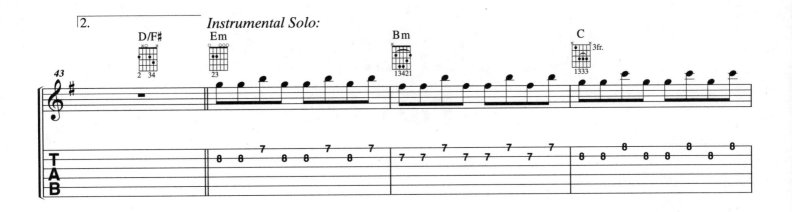

Instrumental Solo:

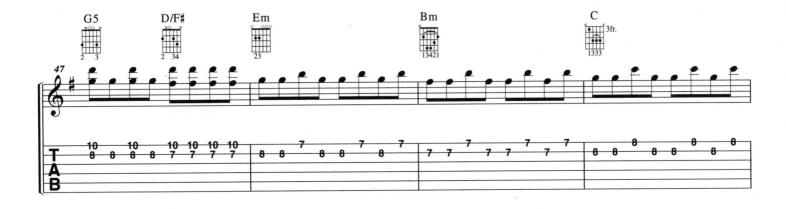

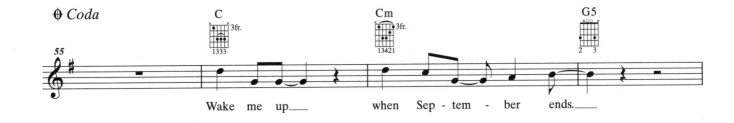

D.C. al Coda

$\oplus$ *Coda*

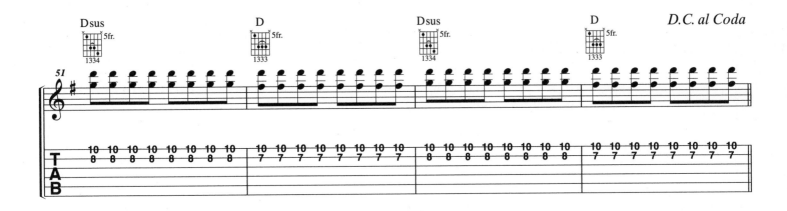

Wake me up___ when Sep - tem - ber ends.___

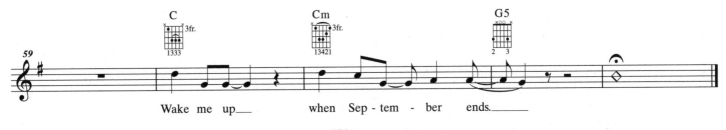

Wake me up___ when Sep - tem - ber ends.___

You Can Leave Your Hat On

Key Thoughts

There have been several great versions of this song. Joe Cocker's version is probably the most well known, but the version by the song's writer, Randy Newman, is our personal favorite. Randy plays the signature riff on the piano, but we've arranged it all for guitar.

Take Note

Below is the signature riff. Use all down-strokes, and mute the strings with your palm to create a constant, driving, eighth-note pulse. The only up-stroke is at the end of the first measure. Use a short, sharp attack to give the up-stroke an abrupt stab. You don't have to hit all four strings on the up-stroke, mostly just the top two.

The introduction is a transcription of the piano part. Listen to Randy's recording before you try to read the music. On the last page of our arrangement, you'll find an optional fingerstyle version of the entire introduction. The fingerstyle version allows you to play it more like the piano version. Your fingers pluck constant eighth-note chords (the piano's right hand), with the signature bass line underneath (the piano's left hand). Try both versions and see which you prefer.

Fun Fact

In addition to being a phenomenal songwriter, Randy Newman is also a prolific film composer. His list of movie scores includes *Toy Story*, *A Bug's Life*, *James and the Giant Peach*, *Cars*, *Avalon*, *Parenthood*, *Seabiscuit*, *The Natural*, *Awakenings*, *Ragtime*, and *Meet the Parents*. Newman's love affair with the movie industry goes beyond just music. In 1986, he collaborated with Steve Martin and Lorne Michaels on the screenplay for the hit comedy *Three Amigos*. Newman wrote three songs for the film and even provided the voice for a singing bush in the movie.

YOU CAN LEAVE YOUR HAT ON

Words and Music by
RANDY NEWMAN

*Refer to last page for an optional fingerstyle version of the introductory piano part.

Mute bottom strings throughout

You Can Leave Your Hat On - 5 - 1

leave your hat on.
You give me a rea-son to live.

You can leave your hat on.
You give me a rea-son to live. You give me a rea-son to live.

1.

You can leave_ your hat on.
You give me a rea-son to live._

2.

Interlude:

D.S. % al Coda

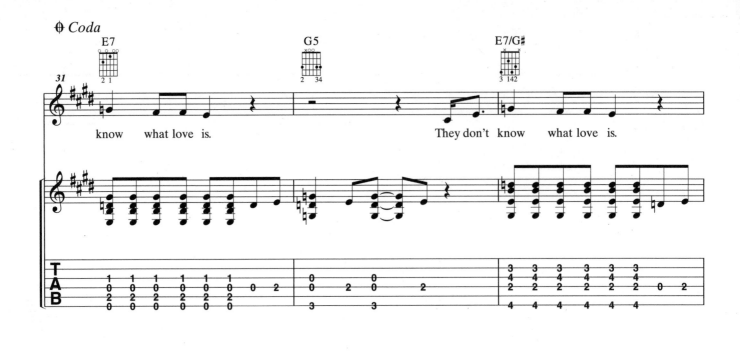

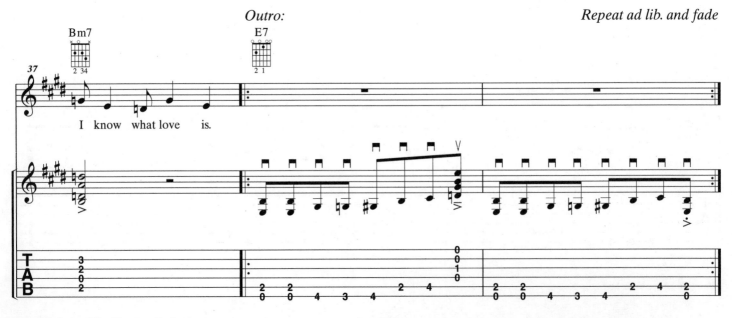

Verse 3:
Suspicious minds are talking,
Try'n' to tear us apart.
They say that my love is wrong,
They don't know what love is.
They don't know what love is.
They don't know what love is.
They don't know what love is.
I know what love is.

Optional fingerstyle arrangement of the introductory piano riff:

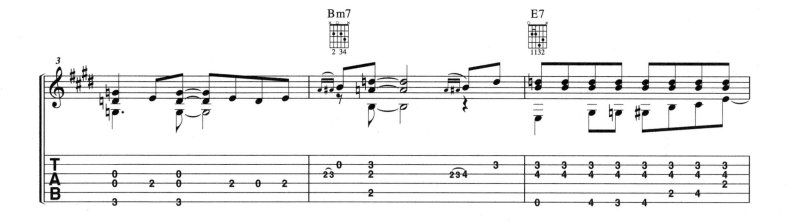

Chord Theory

You don't have to understand the music theory of chord construction to play the songs in this book. The notation, TAB, and chord diagrams tell you everything you need to know to play the music correctly. Someday, though, you're bound to find music that doesn't give you as much information as we have, and you'll need to know at least a little bit about chords to get it right. This section should help you out in those situations, and also add some basic chops to your knowledge of music.

Intervals

Play any note on the guitar, then play a note one fret above it. The distance between these two notes is a *half step*. Play another note followed by a note two frets above it. The distance between these two notes is a *whole step* (two half steps). The distance between any two notes is referred to as an *interval*.

In the example of the C major scale on the following page, the letter names are shown above the notes and the *scale degrees* (numbers) of the notes are written below. Notice that C is the first degree of the scale, D is the second, and so on.

The name of an interval is determined by counting the number of scale degrees from one note to the next. For example, an interval of a 3rd, starting on C, would be determined by counting up three scale degrees, or C–D–E (1–2–3). C to E is a 3rd. An interval of a 4th, starting on C, would be determined by counting up four scale degrees, or C–D–E–F (1–2–3–4). C to F is a 4th.

Intervals are not only labeled by the distance between scale degrees, but by the *quality* of the interval. An interval's quality is determined by counting the number of whole steps and half steps between the two notes of that interval. For example, C to E is a 3rd. C to E is also a *major* third because there are 2 whole steps between C and E. Likewise, C to E♭ is a 3rd. C to E♭ is also a *minor* third because there are 1½ steps between C and E♭.

There are five qualities used to describe intervals: *major*, *minor*, *perfect*, *diminished*, and *augmented*.

Interval Qualities

Quality	Abbreviation
major	M
minor	m
perfect	P
diminished	dim or °
augmented	aug or +

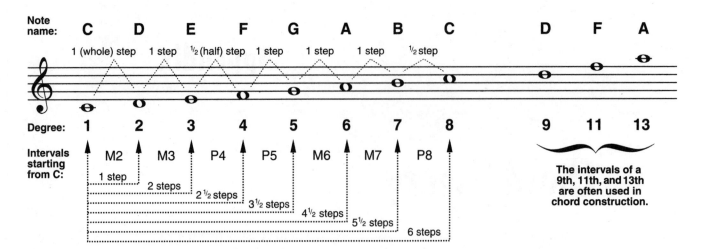

Particular intervals are associated with certain qualities. Not all qualities pertain to every type of interval, as seen in the following table.

Interval Type	Possible Qualities
2nd, 9th	major, minor, augmented
3rd, 6th, 13th	major, minor, diminished, augmented
4th, 5th, 11th	perfect, diminished, augmented
7th	major, minor, diminished

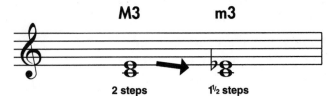

When a major interval is made smaller by a half step, it becomes a minor interval.

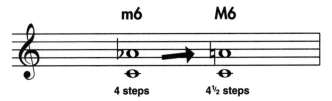

When a minor interval is made larger by a half step, it becomes a major interval.

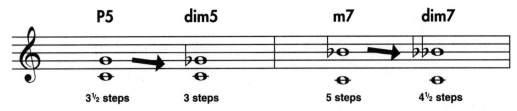

When a perfect or minor interval is made smaller by a half step, it becomes a diminished interval.

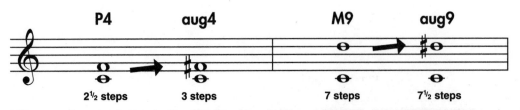

When a perfect or major interval is made larger by a half step, it becomes an augmented interval.

Following is a table of intervals starting on the note C. Notice that some intervals are labeled *enharmonic*, which means that they are written differently but sound the same (see aug2 and m3).

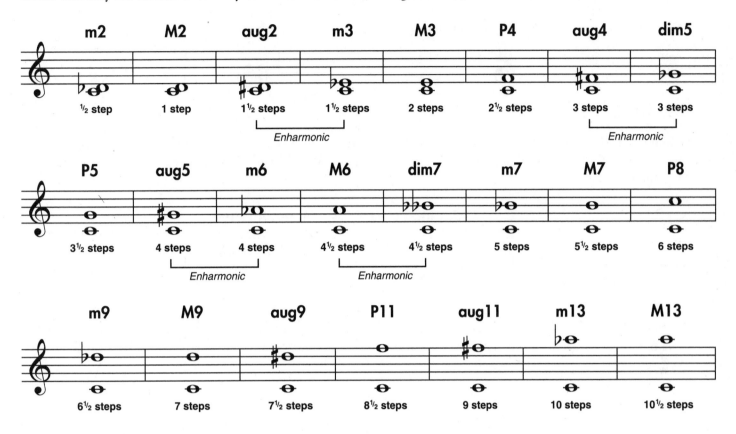

Basic Triads

Two or more notes played together are called a *chord*. Most commonly, a chord will consist of three or more notes. A three-note chord is called a *triad*. The *root* of a triad (or any other chord) is the note from which a chord is constructed. The relationship of the intervals from the root to the other notes of a chord determines the chord *type*. Triads are most frequently identified as one of four chord types: *major*, *minor*, *diminished*, and *augmented*.

Chord Types

All chord types can be identified by the intervals used to create the chord. For example, the C major triad is built beginning with C as the root, adding a major 3rd (E) and adding a perfect 5th (G). All major triads contain a root, M3, and P5.

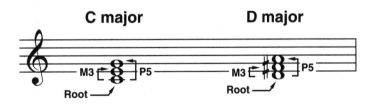

Minor triads contain a root, minor 3rd, and perfect 5th. (An easier way to build a minor triad is to simply lower the 3rd of a major triad.) All minor triads contain a root, m3, and P5.

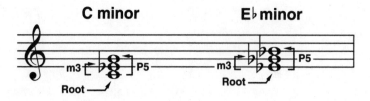

Diminished triads contain a root, minor 3rd, and diminished 5th. If the perfect 5th of a minor triad is made smaller by a half step (to become a diminished 5th), the result is a diminished triad. All diminished triads contain a root, m3, and dim5.

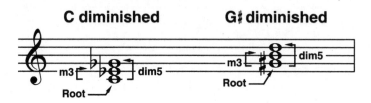

Augmented triads contain a root, major 3rd, and augmented 5th. If the perfect 5th of a major triad is made larger by a half step (to become an augmented 5th), the result is an augmented triad. All augmented triads contain a root, M3, and aug5.

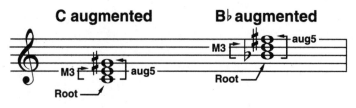

Chord Inversions

An important concept to remember about chords is that the bottom note of a chord will not always be the root. If the root of a triad, for instance, is moved above the 5th so that the 3rd is the bottom note of the chord, it is said to be in the *first inversion*. If the root and 3rd are moved above the 5th, the chord is in the *second inversion*. The number of inversions that a chord can have is related to the number of notes in the chord: a three-note chord can have two inversions, a four-note chord can have three inversions, etc.

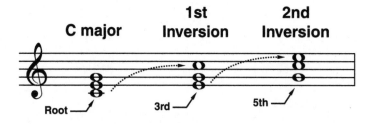

Building Chords

By using the four chord types as basic building blocks, it is possible to create a variety of chords by adding 6ths, 7ths, 9ths, 11ths, and so on. The following are examples of some of the many variations.

C Major Suspended Fourth
Csus

C Flat Fifth
C(♭5)
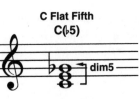

C Major Add Ninth
C(add9)
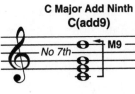

C Diminished
C°
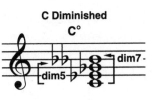

C Major Sixth
C6
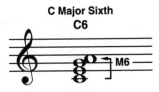

C Sixth Add Ninth
C6/9

C Minor Sixth Add Ninth
Cm6/9
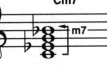

C Minor Sixth
Cm6
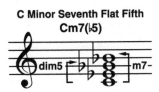

C Seventh
C7
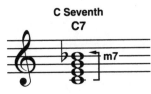

C Seventh Suspended Fourth
C7sus
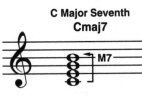

C Minor Seventh
Cm7
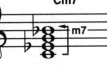

C Minor Seventh Flat Fifth
Cm7(♭5)
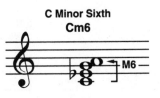

C Seventh Augmented Fifth
C7+
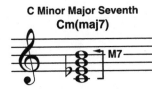

C Seventh Flat Fifth
C7(♭5)
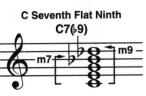

C Major Seventh
Cmaj7
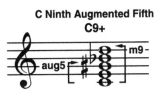

C Major Seventh Flat Fifth
Cmaj7(♭5)
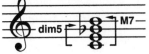

C Minor Major Seventh
Cm(maj7)
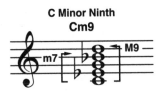

C Seventh Flat Ninth
C7(♭9)
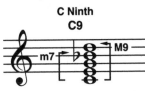

C Seventh Augmented Ninth
C7(♯9)
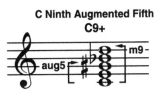

C Seventh Flat Ninth Augmented Fifth
C7+(♭9)

C Minor Ninth
Cm9
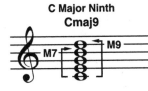

C Ninth
C9
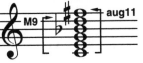

C Ninth Augmented Fifth
C9+

C Ninth Flat Fifth
C9(♭5)
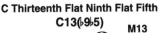

C Major Ninth
Cmaj9
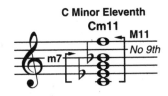

C Ninth Augmented Eleventh
C9(♯11)
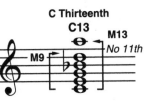

C Minor Ninth Major Seventh
Cm9(maj7)
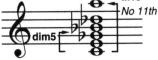

C Eleventh
C11

C Minor Eleventh
Cm11

C Thirteenth
C13

C Thirteenth Flat Ninth
C13(♭9)

C Thirteenth Flat Ninth Flat Fifth
C13(♭9♭5)

So far, the examples provided to illustrate intervals and chord construction have been based on C. Until you're familiar with chords, the C chord examples on the previous page can serve as a guide for building chords based on other notes. For example, to construct a G7(♭9) chord, you can first determine what intervals are contained in C7(♭9) and use the steps below to build the same chord starting on G.

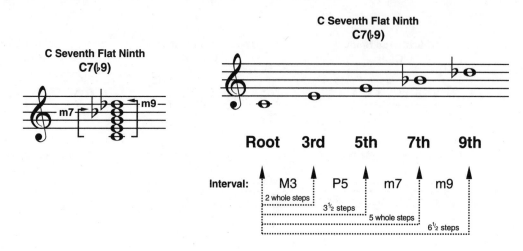

- First, determine the *root* of the chord. A chord is always named for its root, so G is the root of G7(♭9).

- Count *letter names* up from the *letter name of the root* (G) to determine the intervals of the chord. Counting three letter names up from G to B (G–A–B, 1–2–3) is a 3rd, G to D (G–A–B–C–D) is a 5th, G to F is a 7th, and G to A is a 9th.

- Determine the *quality* of the intervals by counting half steps and whole steps up from the root. G to B (2 whole steps) is a major 3rd, G to D (3½ steps) is a perfect 5th, G to F (5 whole steps) is a minor 7th, and G to A♭ (6½ steps) is a minor 9th.

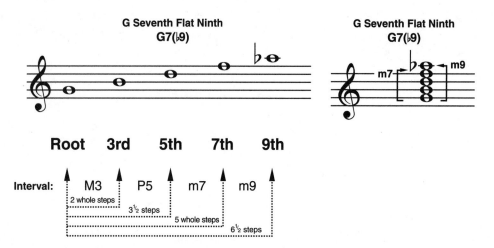

Follow this general guideline for determining the notes of any chord. As interval and chord construction become more familiar to you, you'll be able to create original fingerings on the guitar. Don't be afraid to experiment!

The Circle of Fifths

The *circle of fifths* will help to clarify which chords are enharmonic equivalents (yes, chords can be written enharmonically as well as notes). The circle of fifths also serves as a quick reference guide to the relationship of the keys and how key signatures can be figured out in a logical manner. Moving clockwise (up a P5) provides all of the sharp keys by progressively adding one sharp to the key signature. Moving counter-clockwise (down a P5) provides the flat keys by progressively adding one flat to the key signature.

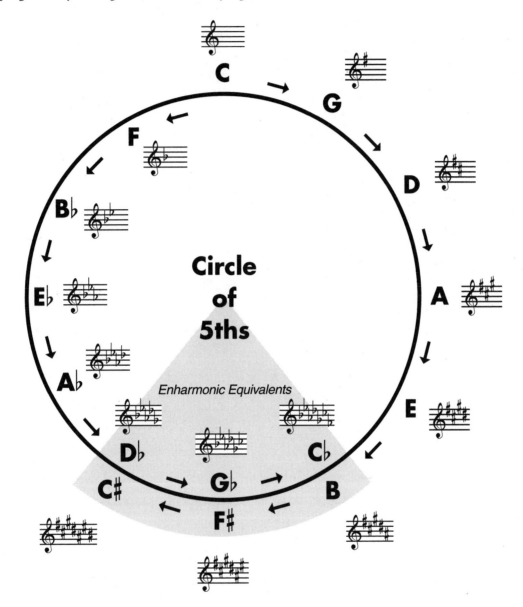

Chord Symbol Variations

Chord symbols are a form of musical shorthand that provide you with as much information about a chord as quickly as possible. The intent of using chord symbols is to convey enough information to recognize the chord, yet not so much as to confuse the meaning of the symbol. Chord symbols are not universally standardized and are written in many different ways—some are easy to understand, others are confusing. To illustrate this point, following is a list of some of the variations copyists, composers, and arrangers have created for the more common chord symbols.

C	Csus	C(♭5)	C(add9)	C5	Cm
C major	Csus4	C-5	C(9)	C(no3)	Cmin
Cmaj	C(addF)	C(5-)	C(add2)	C(omit3)	Cmi
CM	C4	C(#4)	C(+9)		C-
			C(+D)		

C+	C°	C6	C6/9	Cm6/9	Cm6
C+5	Cdim	Cmaj6	C6(add9)	C-6/9	C-6
Caug	Cdim7	C(addA)	C6(addD)	Cm6(+9)	Cm(addA)
Caug5	C7dim	C(A)	C9(no7)	Cm6(add9)	Cm(+6)
C(#5)			C9/6	Cm6(+D)	

C7	C7sus	Cm7	Cm7(♭5)	C7+	C7(♭5)
C(addB♭)	C7sus4	Cmi7	Cmi7-5	C7+5	C7-5
C7̶	Csus7	Cmin7	C-7(5-)	C7aug	C7(5-)
C(-7)	C7(+4)	C-7	Cø	C7aug5	C7̶-5
C(+7)		C7mi	C ½dim	C7(#5)	C7(#4)

Cmaj7	Cmaj7(♭5)	Cm(maj7)	C7(♭9)	C7(#9)	C7+(♭9)
Cma7	Cmaj7(-5)	C-maj7	C7(-9)	C7(+9)	Caug7-9
C7̶	C7̶(-5)	C-7̶	C9♭	C9#	C+7(♭9)
CΔ	CΔ(♭5)	Cmi7̶	C9-	C9+	C+9♭
CΔ7					C7+(-9)

Cm9	C9	C9+	C9(♭5)	Cmaj9	C9(#11)
Cm7(9)	C_7^9	C9(+5)	C9(-5)	C7̶(9)	C9(+11)
Cm7(+9)	C7add9	Caug9	$C7_{-5}^9$	C7̶(+9)	C(#11)
C-9	C7(addD)	C(#9#5)	C9(5♭)	C9(maj7)	C11+
Cmi7(9+)	C7(+9)	C+9		C9̶	C11#

Cm9(maj7)	C11	Cm11	C13	C13(♭9)	C13($^{♭9}_{♭5}$)
C-9(#7)	C9(11)	C-11	C9addA	C13(-9)	C13(-9-5)
C(-9)7̶	C9addF	Cm(♭11)	C9(6)	$C_{♭9}^{13}$	C(♭9♭5)addA
Cmi9(#7)	C9+11	$Cmi7_9^{11}$	C7addA	C(♭9)addA	
	$C7_{11}^9$	$C-7(_{11}^9)$	C7+A		

166

Reading Chord Frames

Guitar chord frames are diagrams that show the fingering and position of a particular chord on the neck of the guitar. Vertical lines represent the strings, and horizontal lines represent the frets. Dots on the diagram show exactly where to place the fingers, and corresponding numbers at the bottom of the frame tell which fingers to use.

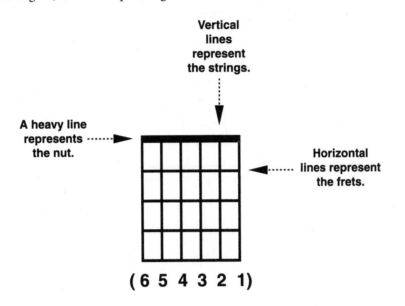

Vertical lines represent the strings.

A heavy line represents the nut.

Horizontal lines represent the frets.

(6 5 4 3 2 1)

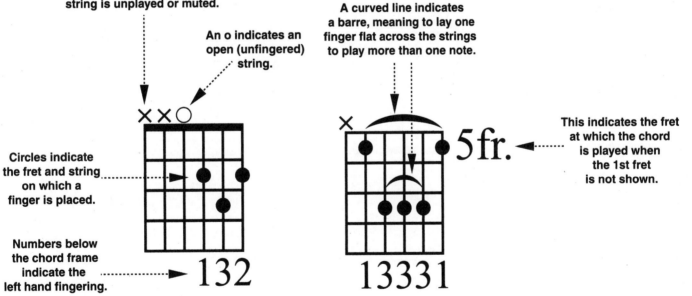

An x indicates that the string is unplayed or muted.

An o indicates an open (unfingered) string.

A curved line indicates a barre, meaning to lay one finger flat across the strings to play more than one note.

Circles indicate the fret and string on which a finger is placed.

This indicates the fret at which the chord is played when the 1st fret is not shown.

Numbers below the chord frame indicate the left hand fingering.

132

13331

5fr.

Guitar Fingerboard Chart

Frets 1–12

STRINGS

	6th	5th	4th	3rd	2nd	1st
	E	A	D	G	B	E

FRETS	6th	5th	4th	3rd	2nd	1st
← Open →	E	A	D	G	B	E
← 1st Fret →	F	A#/B♭	D#/E♭	G#/A♭	C	F
← 2nd Fret →	F#/G♭	B	E	A	C#/D♭	F#/G♭
← 3rd Fret →	G	C	F	A#/B♭	D	G
← 4th Fret →	G#/A♭	C#/D♭	F#/G♭	B	D#/E♭	G#/A♭
← 5th Fret →	A	D	G	C	E	A
← 6th Fret →	A#/B♭	D#/E♭	G#/A♭	C#/D♭	F	A#/B♭
← 7th Fret →	B	E	A	D	F#/G♭	B
← 8th Fret →	C	F	A#/B♭	D#/E♭	G	C
← 9th Fret →	C#/D♭	F#/G♭	B	E	G#/A♭	C#/D♭
← 10th Fret →	D	G	C	F	A	D
← 11th Fret →	D#/E♭	G#/A♭	C#/D♭	F#/G♭	A#/B♭	D#/E♭
← 12th Fret →	E	A	D	G	B	E

Fretboard note names (strings 6th 5th 4th 3rd 2nd 1st = E A D G B E):

Fret	6th	5th	4th	3rd	2nd	1st
1st	F	A#/B♭	D#/E♭	G#/A♭	C	F
2nd	F#/G♭	B	E	A	C#/D♭	F#/G♭
3rd	G	C	F	A#/B♭	D	G
4th	G#/A♭	C#/D♭	F#/G♭	B	D#/E♭	G#/A♭
5th	A	D	G	C	E	A
6th	A#/B♭	D#/E♭	G#/A♭	C#/D♭	F	A#/B♭
7th	B	E	A	D	F#	B
8th	C	F	A#/B♭	D#/E♭	G	C
9th	C#/D♭	F#/G♭	B	E	G#/A♭	C#/D♭
10th	D	G	C	F	A	D
11th	D#/E♭	G#/A♭	C#/D♭	F#/G♭	A#/B♭	D#/E♭
12th	E	A	D	G	B	E

Glossary

accent   Emphasis on a beat, note, or chord.

accidental   A sharp, flat, or natural sign that occurs in a measure.

altered tuning   Any tuning other than standard tuning on the guitar.

arpeggio   The notes of a chord played one after another instead of simultaneously.

bar   See *measure (or bar)*.

bar line   A vertical line that indicates where one measure ends and another begins.

barre   To fret multiple strings with one finger.

barre chord   A chord played by fretting several strings with one finger.

bend   A technique of pushing a guitar string up or down with the fretting finger to change the pitch.

bridge   The part of the guitar that anchors the strings to the body.

brush stroke   To lightly strum the guitar strings with the index finger of the right hand.

capo   A device placed around the neck of the guitar to raise the pitch of the strings.

Carter style   A guitar technique, named after Maybelle Carter of the Carter family, that combines rhythm strumming and single-note melody playing.

chord   A group of three or more notes played simultaneously.

chord progression   A sequence of chords played in succession.

common time   The most common time signature in music; there are four beats to every measure and the quarter note gets one beat. Same as $\frac{4}{4}$.

countermelody   A melody played at the same time as the main melody.

cut time   A time signature that usually indicates a faster tempo where there are two beats to every measure and the half note gets one beat. Same as $\frac{2}{2}$.

dotted note   A note followed by a dot, indicating that the length of the note is longer by one half of the note's original length.

double bar line   A sign made of one thin line and one thick line, indicating the end of a piece of music.

double stop   A group of two notes played simultaneously.

downbeat   The first beat of a measure.

down-pick   To pick the string downward, toward the floor.

down-stroke   To strike the strings downward, toward the floor.

down-strum   To strum the strings downward, toward the floor.

drop D tuning   An altered tuning in which the 6th string of the guitar is lowered from E to D.

economy of motion   A concept for efficient playing that involves moving as few fingers as little as possible when changing chords.

eighth note   A note equal to half a quarter note, or one half beat in $\frac{4}{4}$ time.

eighth rest   A rest equal to the duration of an eighth note.

fermata   A symbol that indicates to hold a note for about twice as long as usual.

fifth   The fifth note of a scale above the root note, the distance of seven half steps.

fingerboard   See *fretboard.*

fingerpicking   A style of playing that uses the right hand fingers to pluck the guitar strings rather than using a pick.

fingerstyle   To play the strings with the fingers of the right hand rather than using a pick.

flat   A symbol that indicates to lower a note one half step.

fret   The metal strips across the fretboard of a guitar.

fretboard   The part of the guitar neck where the frets lay.

G clef   See *treble clef.*

groove   The sense of rhythm in a piece of music.

half note   A note equal to two quarter notes, or two beats in $\frac{4}{4}$ time.

half rest   A rest equal to the duration of a half note.

half step   The distance of one fret on the guitar.

hammer-on   A technique by which a note is made to sound after playing the string with the right hand by tapping down on the string with another finger of the fretting hand.

harmonics   The notes of the harmonic series that sound clear and bell-like when played, produced by lightly touching a string at various points on the fretboard and indicated in notation with diamond-shaped symbols.

harmony   The result of two or more tones played simultaneously.

interval   The distance in pitch between notes.

key   The tonal center of a piece of music.

key signature   The group of sharps or flats that appears at the beginning of a piece of music to indicate what key the music is in.

ledger lines   Short horizontal lines used to extend a staff either higher or lower.

major chord   A chord consisting of a root, a major third, and a perfect fifth.

major scale   The most common scale in music, consisting of a specific order of whole and half steps: W-W-H-W-W-W-H.

major third   A note that is four half steps up from the root.

measure (or bar)   Divisions of the staff that are separated by bar lines and contain equal numbers of beats.

minor chord   A chord consisting of a root, a minor third, and a perfect fifth.

minor third   A note that is three half steps up from the root.

mode   A set of notes arranged into a specific scale.

mute   To stop a note from ringing on the guitar by placing either the right or left hand over the strings.

natural   A symbol that indicates a note is not sharp or flat.

note   A symbol used to represent a musical tone.

nut   The part of the guitar at the top of the neck that aligns the strings over the fretboard.

octave   The interval between two immediate notes of the same name, equivalent to 12 frets on the guitar, or eight scale steps.

open E tuning   An altered tuning for the guitar in which the strings are tuned from low to high E-B-E-G♯-B-E.

open position   Fingering for chords that incorporates open strings and no barre.

palm mute   A technique of muffling the guitar strings with the right hand palm at the bridge of the guitar.

pick   A device used to pluck or strum the strings of a guitar.

pima   Abbreviations for the right hand fingers in fingerpicking notation, in which *p* = thumb, *i* = index finger, *m* = middle finger, and *a* = ring finger.

pinch technique   A fingerpicking technique in which the right hand plucks two strings at once between the thumb and another finger.

pitch   The location of a note related to its lowness or highness.

position   The location of the hand on the fretboard at a particular fret.

pull-off   A technique in which two notes are fingered on the same string, and the lower note is then made to sound by pulling the fretting finger off the higher note.

quarter note   A note equal to one beat in $\frac{4}{4}$ time; the basic unit of musical time.

quarter rest   A rest equal to the duration of a quarter note.

repeat signs   A group of various symbols indicating sections of music to be played over again.

rest   A symbol representing measured silence in music.

rhythm   The musical organization of beats.

riff   A short, repeated melodic pattern.

root note   The fundamental note of a chord, and also the note that gives the chord its letter name. The root is the first note of the corresponding major scale.

scale   A set of notes arranged in a specific order of whole steps and half steps. The most common scale is the major scale.

sharp   A symbol that indicates to raise a note one half step.

shuffle rhythm   A rhythm in which eighth notes are played in an uneven, long-short manner.

sixteenth note   A note equal to half an eighth note, or one quarter beat in $\frac{4}{4}$ time.

sixteenth rest   A rest equal to the duration of a sixteenth note.

slide   1. A technique of moving smoothly from one note to another. A note is fingered by the left hand and played by the right hand, then the left hand finger maintains pressure while sliding quickly on the string to the next note without interrupting the sound or picking the note again. Indicated in notation with a diagonal line between notes. 2. A metal or glass tube that fits over a left hand finger, used to fret the strings and produce slide notes.

staccato   To play notes in a short, distinct manner. Indicated in notation by a dot directly over or under the note or chord.

staff   The horizontal lines and spaces upon which music notes are placed to designate their pitch.

standard tuning   The normal tuning for the guitar in which the strings are tuned from low to high E-A-D-G-B-E.

strum   To play several strings by brushing quickly across them with a pick or the fingers.

swing   To play eighth notes in an uneven, long-short rhythm.

syncopation   A shift of rhythmic emphasis to the weak beat, or to a weak part of a beat.

TAB   Abbreviation for *tablature*.

tablature   A system of guitar notation that uses a graphic representation of the six strings of the guitar with numbers indicating which fret to play.

tempo   The speed at which music is played.

tie   A curved line that joins two or more notes of the same pitch, indicating to play them as one continuous note.

time signature   A sign resembling a fraction that appears at the beginning of a piece of music. The top number indicates how many beats are in each measure and the bottom number indicates what kind of note gets one beat.

Travis picking   A picking technique, named for country guitarist Merle Travis, in which the right thumb plays constant notes alternating between two strings.

treble clef   A symbol at the beginning of the staff that designates the second line as the note G. Also called the *G clef*.

triplet   A group of three notes played in the time of two.

unison   The same pitch played at the same time on different strings of the guitar.

up-pick   To pick the string upward, toward the ceiling.

up-stroke   To strike the strings upward, toward the ceiling.

up-strum   To strum the strings upward, toward the ceiling.

whole note   A note equal to four quarter notes, or four beats in $\frac{4}{4}$ time.

whole rest   A rest equal to the duration of a whole note, or the duration of any full measure.

whole step   The distance of two frets on the guitar.

The following blank chord frames and staff systems may be used to keep track of new chords, songs, and riffs. Write them here as you learn so you won't forget them.

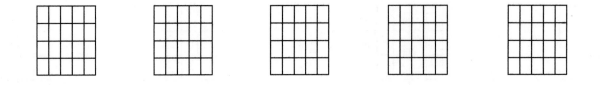

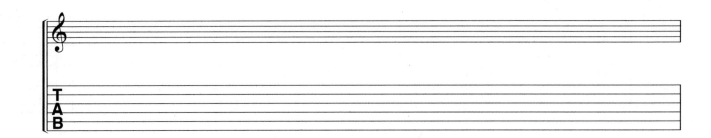

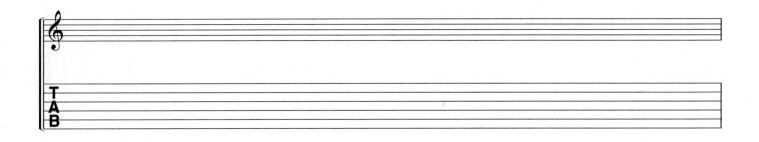

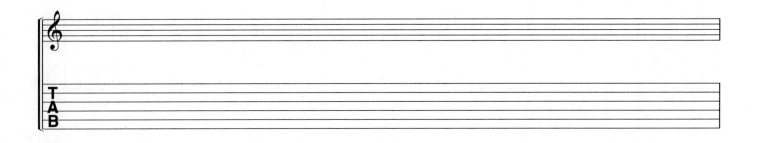

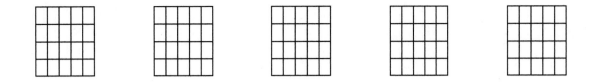

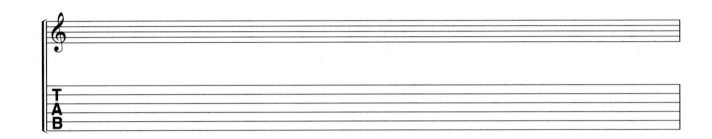

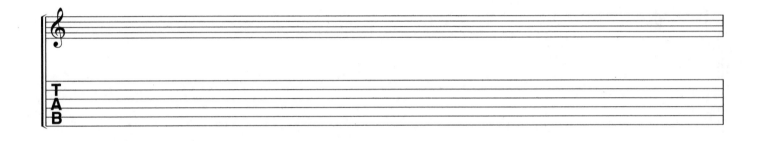

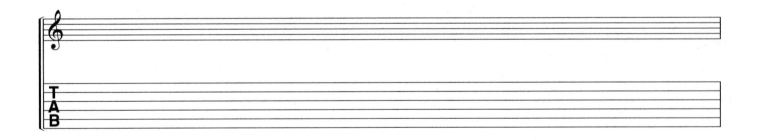

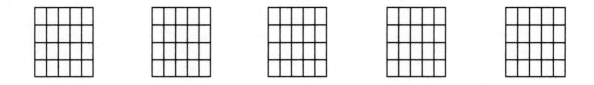

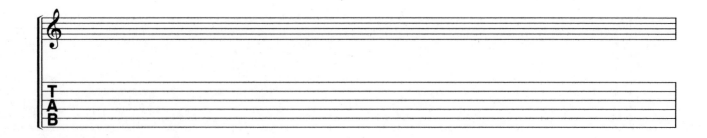

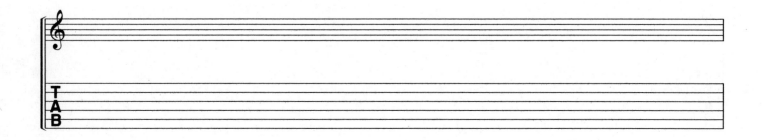

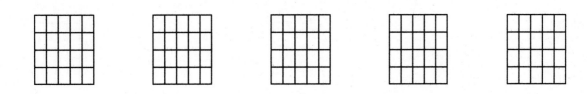

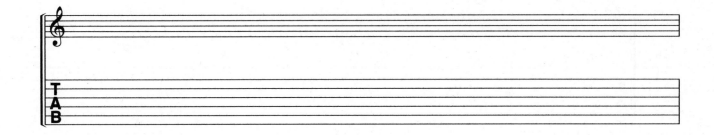

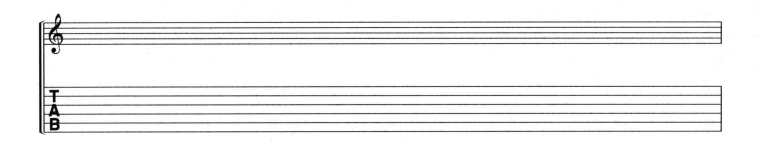

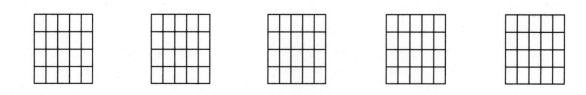

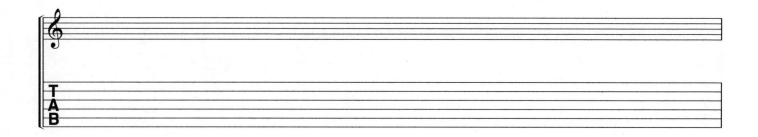

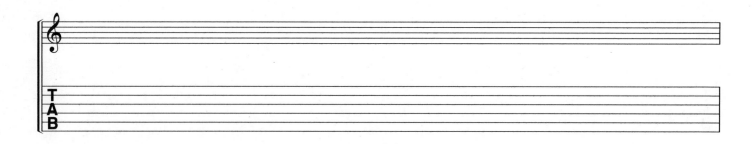

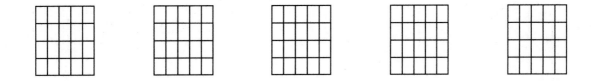

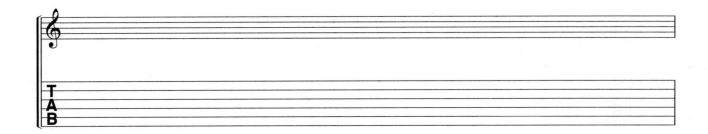

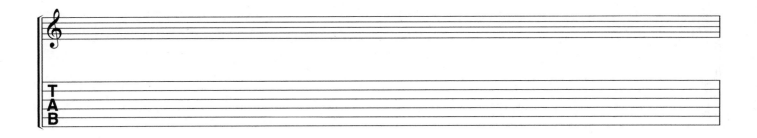

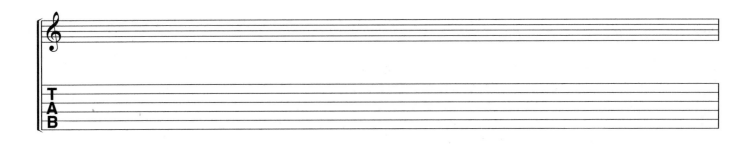

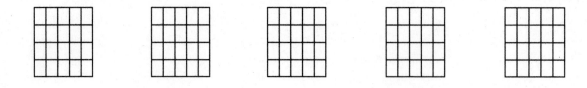

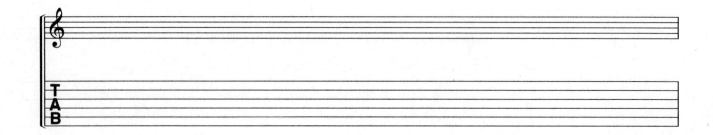

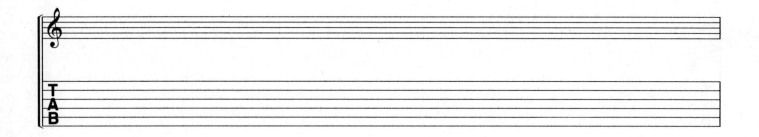

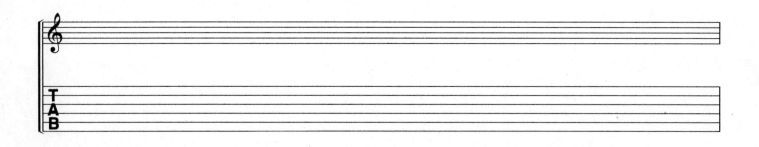